HRLF
Human Resource Leadership Forum
HR. Brilliantly.

Enjoy this book compliments of HRLF

www.hrlf.org

Thank you for attending

HR Strategy and Millennial Engagement

Praise for *What Millennials Want from Work*

"The workforce of today is more diverse, complex, and challenging than ever before. Over the next 10 years, organizations big and small may succeed or fail based on how they embrace the Millennial generation. This book provides valuable insights and tools that can help us understand what's inside this cohort and how we can unlock their unique value."

—Scott Pitasky, Executive Vice President and Chief Partner Resource Officer, Starbucks

"If you think you understand the Millennials in your life, think again. In this new generational research, Deal and Levenson offer some new twists on what Millennials want, think, and do, and how organizations can maximize their engagement and contribution. As a Millennial manager, parent, and talent practitioner, the global perspective and practical recommendations in *What Millennials Want from Work* have already influenced my thinking."

—Mary Eckenrod, Vice President, Global Talent Management, Johnson Controls

"This book will help you reinvent the way you inspire and connect with Millennials. Anyone looking to truly understand this exciting and complex generation will benefit from Deal and Levenson's ability to resolve seemingly contradictory paradoxes. Think of it as a generational decoder key, giving you simple secrets to deeply engage and bring out the best of Millennials' passion to constantly learn, grow, and make a meaningful difference."

—Eva Sage Gavin, Vice Chair, Skills for America's Future,
The Aspen Institute; Senior Advisor, Boston Consulting Group;
and former EVP, Human Resources and Corporate Affairs, Gap Inc.

"This is an outstanding resource that you can use right now to engage Millennials and propel your business forward. Deal and Levenson provide an incredibly rich, practical picture of what really drives Millennials and how to engage, lead, and work with them to mutually benefit your bottom line. *What Millennials Want from Work* will help you win the war for the talent you need for innovation and long-term growth."

—Steve Milovich, Senior Vice President, Global Human Resources,
Disney ABC Television, The Walt Disney Company

"Organizations everywhere can benefit from the sharp insights shared in *What Millennials Want from Work*. Debunking common misconceptions, Deal and Levenson provide useful tips for leaders, managers, and coworkers on how to engage and motivate Millennials. They are the future of our workplace, and this book will help everyone who works with Millennials leverage the best they have to offer."

—Anne Hill, Senior Vice President and Chief Human Resources Officer, Avery Dennison

"The state-of-the-art guide to managing and working with Millennials. Based on their extensive research with organizations around the world, Deal and Levenson resolve the debates about whether Millennials are entitled or hardworking, needy or independent, high-tech or high-touch, and disloyal or committed. This data-driven book is full of practical recommendations."

—Adam Grant, Wharton Professor of Management and
New York Times bestselling author of *Give and Take* and *Originals*

"Most pundits treat Millennials like they are a completely different species, relying on anecdotes and trite commentary. Deal and Levenson take a different approach, using scientific analysis to provide data-based insights and separate myth from the real changes happening in our society. The disparity across countries is particularly enlightening. Not only does culture eat strategy for lunch, apparently generational generalities are an appetizer!"

—Tony Sarsam, Chief Executive Officer, Ready Pac Foods

"*What Millenials Want from Work* is for all leaders who want to 'future proof' their talent management skills and strategy. Deal and Levenson have taken their thorough, global research to create a cogent handbook for successfully leading and managing our next generation of talent. The messages are clear, the advice is practical, and the bottom line is inspiring. The choice for current leaders is critical and could define our legacy. We can either nurture and catalyze this dynamic or be disrupted by it, as this new cohort emerges to lead the next generation of talent."

—Jonathan Donner, Vice President,
Global Learning and Capability Development, Unilever

"Just about everyone has opinions on the Millennials in our workforce. But exceptional research that helps us understand what really makes this generation tick has been lacking—until now. Deal and Levenson perform a great service for senior executives everywhere, replacing myths with fresh, candid insights that will help organizations unlock the full potential of their emerging talent."

—John D. Butler, former Executive Vice President
and Chief Human Resource Officer, Textron Inc.

"To understand the future, we must know what drives Millennials, the generation that will lead and shape the next phase of the world's history. This book is an excellent resource, packed with real insights and practical recommendations that are guaranteed to be of high value to all leaders, boardrooms, governments, marketers, educators and parents alike."

—Dennis Finn, Global CEO, Advisian

"Deal and Levenson have comprehensively separated fact from urban myth when it comes to what Millennials want from work. A must-read for anyone interested in ensuring their organization is maximizing execution through higher levels of Millennial engagement and commitment."

—Mark Blankenship, Executive Vice President and
Chief People, Culture, and Corporate Strategy Officer, Jack in the Box

"With rich data and storytelling, Deal and Levenson show us something that we did not know conclusively until now: Millennials are often driven by similar passions and goals, no matter where they live and work in the world. How can global organizations harness their talent? This book offers the smart, practical advice we need to build outstanding leadership pipelines in every corner of the globe."

—Ingar Skaug, retired President and
Group Chief Executive Officer, Wilh. Wilhelmsen ASA

"Millennials are our future. If you manage Millennials or if you are one, read Deal and Levenson's guide to understanding this unique generation. Based on critical global research, this book describes what motivates them and how to adjust your thinking and management style to bring out the best in your whole team!"

—Marshall Goldsmith, author or editor of 35 books,
including the #1 *New York Times* bestselling *Triggers* and
global bestsellers *MOJO* and *What Got You Here Won't Get You There*

"Millennials are smart, talented, and ambitious—and often misunderstood by those of us responsible for developing them. The authors have delivered the kind of engaging, data-driven study about this generation that we've needed for years. With strong analysis and step-by-step guidance, this book will make the conversations that organizations have about cultivating their future leaders far more productive."

—Martin Schneider, Vice President and Global CIO, VF Corporation

"The authors take us on a captivating trip around the world, exploring the many ways in which Millennials are the same and also the fewer but crucial ways in which they differ culturally. For organizations that are truly serious about leveraging world-class research to develop a new generation of global leaders, this book needs to be read now."

—Om Bhatt, former Chairman, State Bank of India

"This book by Deal and Levenson is a must-read for business leaders and HR professionals who want to meet the challenges of attracting, retaining, and rewarding Millennials at work."

—Jacqueline Yew, Senior Vice President, Organizational Strategy and Leadership Development, Pactera Technology International Limited

"Deal and Levenson have done us all a great service. They unpack in a clear and considered way *What Millennials Want from Work* and provide thoughtful and useful tools for engaging this cohort of workers. The greater service is that this is really a book about how to manage anyone in your workforce: Baby Boomers, Gen Y, any generation. Deal and Levenson help us think more holistically about the people who are in our organizations, showing how to get the most out of diverse teams and ensure everyone is included and motivated."

—Laura Liswood, Secretary General, Council of Women World Leaders; Senior Advisor, Goldman Sachs; and author of *The Loudest Duck: Moving Beyond Diversity*

"Deal and Levenson provide profound insights into who Millennials are, what they want, and how they are different culturally around the world. Understanding Millennials is essential to any corporation that wants to succeed both locally and globally. This book provides the guidance and advice on how to manage Millennials your organization needs to grow sustainably."

—Anne Patricia Sutanto, Vice CEO of PT. Pan Brothers Tbk

"Global organizations know that culture can make or break a business model. Today's Millennial generation represents one of the largest cultural challenges, one that can be a catalyst for success or a barrier to realizing global ambitions. Deal and Levenson provide a masterful guide to understanding how much Millennials are driven by similar passions and desires worldwide, and where cultural differences really matter."

—Nenad Pacek, Founder and President, Global Success Advisors GmbH, and Co-founder and Co-CEO, CEEMEA Business Group

"A successful strategy of winning with your customers starts with engaging your own staff. This practical and insightful guide shows how to win with your Millennial staff, and what drives their behavior and decisions. A useful—and fun—read for all leaders who want their organizations to remain relevant and competitive."

—Raimund Snyders, CEO, Mutual & Federal

"Leading an Indian-owned business in a mature industry in a mature region—steel in Europe—I see both the power of Millennials and their impact on the Indian economy. Millennials have the potential both to accelerate the next phase of development of the world's emerging markets and to redesign the future of manufacturing excellence in Europe and throughout the world's mature markets. Deal and Levenson provide a clear road map to follow for leaders who want to enable Millennials' contribution to transform the future."

—Dr. Karl Köhler, CEO and Managing Director, Tata Steel - Europe

WHAT MILLENNIALS WANT FROM WORK

HOW TO MAXIMIZE ENGAGEMENT IN TODAY'S WORKFORCE

JENNIFER J. DEAL   **ALEC LEVENSON**

New York Chicago San Francisco Athens London Madrid
Mexico City Milan New Delhi Singapore Sydney Toronto

2 3 4 5 6 7 8 9 0   QFR/QFR   1 2 1 0 9 8 7 6

ISBN   978-0-07-184267-9
MHID   0-07-184267-5

e-ISBN   978-0-07-184332-4
e-MHID   0-07-184332-9

McGraw-Hill Education books are available at special quantity discounts to use as premiums and sales promotions, or for use in corporate training programs. To contact a representative, please visit the Contact Us page at www.mhprofessional.com.

Library of Congress Cataloging-in-Publication Data

Deal, Jennifer J.
  What millennials want from work : how to maximize engagement in today's workforce / Jennifer Deal and Alec Levenson.
     pages cm
  Includes bibliographical references.
  ISBN 978-0-07-184267-9 (alk. paper) — ISBN 0-07-184267-5 (alk. paper) 1.   Generation Y—Employment. 2.   Conflict of generations in the workplace. 3.   Intergenerational relations. 4.   Personnel management. I. Levenson, Alec Robert, 1966- author. II. Title.
  HF5549.5.C75.D43 2016
     658.3—dc23   2015032697

For G, M, & D

and

*for E, C, E, A, & E, who will be the subject of
discussion ten years from now*

and

*in honor of our families of post-2000 kids, Millennials, Gen Xers,
Boomers, Silent Generation, World War II Generation,
and Lost Generation. They are a constant reminder to
us that dedication and effort transcend both generation
and age. We are grateful every day for their gifts.*

CONTENTS

FOREWORD

We are all fascinated by intergenerational differences—and probably no more so than in Millennials. Are they really that different from any other demographic group, and if so, what is the source of these differences and what should this mean for those who support, manage, and lead them? It is no surprise that this fascination has created endless analysis of this generation's current work habits and motivations and indeed much speculation about its future aspirations and likely career trajectories. Much of this analysis is simply based on relatively narrow observations and is often tinged with a strong personal belief of the observer. Some of it is negative and stereotypical.

That's why the studies that form the backbone of this book are so important. Over many thousands of hours of interviews, through state-of-the-art social platform conversations, and with global in-depth surveys, the research team began to tease out the underlying reality of being a Millennial. They listened to how Millennials saw the world, whether they were in Tokyo or Boston, Shanghai or Buenos Aires. They heard their descriptions of their world as Millennials saw it and the reality of their everyday choices and decisions.

What has emerged is an extraordinary insight into what it means to be a young person in today's industrial world. Some insights were highly predictable. There is no doubt that technology has shaped the lives of this generation from birth and will continue to do so. Millennials are so familiar and at ease with cyberspace that their relationships are formed and supported in this way. This is a generation that entered the job market during the recession of 2007, so it's no surprise that working hard and getting ahead are important to them. Other insights were less expected. Contrary to general perceptions, while this generation may job-hop for higher pay, they are committed to the company they work for and keen to make a contribution. They do care about the wider world, but as many are saddled with significant debt, the here-and-now compensation is also important to them. They don't want to enter their middle age still in debt, and they want to be sure they have made sufficient savings for their old age. And while they have grown up in a technologically enhanced world, they realize and appreciate the charm of working face-to-face and care a lot about the social communities they create at work.

This research has captured this generation in a moment of time. We see Millennials experiencing their day-to-day lives, looking back to the paths that brought them here, and looking forward to what could lie ahead. Work is fundamental to their lives, and the quality of work that they are engaged in is crucial to their satisfaction and their feelings of well-being. As they look out across a long working life, they realize that they are building the foundations of skills and competencies and are aware of the importance of how they achieve this. They know that being a lifelong learner will be crucial and are willing to make the investments at this early stage of their working lives. Listening to their views on work, it is clear what the management tasks are: to provide work that is interesting and worthwhile, to give feedback that is frequent and insightful, to trust them to do good work and to have some autonomy over the way they do it, and to ensure that their voices are heard. Listening to their views, what is also clear is the corrosive impact that current organizational practices have on them: many report the frustration of working long hours in tasks that seem unconnected to the mission of the organization, others the heavy weight of bureaucracy on their shoulders, and some speak of being bullied at work.

As the research team members began to piece together the insights from the various methods they used, it was clear that the narrative they developed would have to be a great deal more sophisticated than a simple description.

This and/and orientation is obvious from the way Millennials describe their wider life. The members of this cohort have now joined the workforce and are beginning to make the choices that will shape some of the life that lies ahead of them. Perhaps for previous generations—certainly for a Baby Boomer like me—that would have been sufficient. It was work or home. But very early in the research, the team realized that members of this generation viewed their life in a much more integrated way. For example, it is not going to be either work *or* home life—it is going to be work *and* home. In a sense, that simple shift is the narrative that unites much of what the research team found. This is a generation whose members still live with their parents at a greater rate than previous generations did. They see themselves as very much part of the family unit and, as they look forward, see their own family playing a central role in their life. The parents of this generation struggled to create this unity between work and home. The Millennials understand and acknowledge this, and many have made the resolution of this struggle and the creation of unity a central plank of their approach to work. Their work is important to them—but so too is the time they give to keep themselves healthy and happy, the contributions they make to their neighborhoods and local communities, and the role they play in addressing some of the bigger global issues the world faces.

Much of the previous descriptions of the lives of Millennials had taken as the context the life of those in the West. This narrow focus takes away from a fundamental aspect of this generation. That is why the global reach of this research is so crucial. We are witness to the first globally connected generation in which social media and the ubiquity of global entertainment and education have erased many national differences. Talking to the educated Millennials in Mumbai, London, or Boston, many of the same themes emerge. This is a generation that is truly global. Millennials around the world share many of the same attitudes, and many are interested in the world outside of their country boundaries and value an opportunity to work in other parts of the world.

The study is fortunate in its ability to look across countries. It is also fortunate to have heard the voices of both women and men. This gender balance is crucial because this generation is party to a fundamental transformation in the way that men and women engage in work. Many of those who are in partnerships are already experiencing the day-to-day realities of managing a dual career, and those with small children are juggling their working lives in a way that their parents did not. As the roles of men and women at work and in the home transform, this is a generation with very few role models to show the way ahead. Through their stories, we can learn what it is to be a pioneer and how they are thinking about making the choices that will give them the foundation for their home lives over the coming decades. For previous generations, working flexibly was something unusual, often given as a reward. For members of this generation, creating the lives they want demands more autonomy and more flexibility.

This is a generation that has a perspective on the world it has inherited. Millennials understand the role that corporations play and believe that the work they do and the corporations they work for should make a wider contribution. Indeed, the choice they make about which corporation to join is influenced by the corporation's history of social responsibility and contribution to the community. They have glimpsed the resource and climate change issues that they face, and know that working collaboratively with multiple stakeholders will be key to making change happen. They are looking beyond their immediate workplace to make a difference. It is they who will be faced with building a world that is sustainable for the generations that follow them. They want to do this by building their own competence and then reaching out. It is this generation that will be called upon to work collaboratively and globally in a way that has never been done before.

As we stand with the members of this generation at this point in time, what we have learned is that those who manage and lead them have an extraordinary duty of stewardship. A duty to understand more deeply what it is that members of this generation place at the front of their decision making. A duty to build a context in which they can flourish and reach their full potential. And a duty to mentor and support them to navigate what is ahead of them. Many of the people in this study will rise to managerial roles responsible for the working lives of hundreds of people. Some will become the leaders of tomorrow's large corporations, while others will move into entrepreneurial roles. We are glimpsing the leaders of tomorrow. By understanding them more deeply and empathizing with them more profoundly, we can support them to become the leaders our world needs.

Lynda Gratton
Professor of Management Practice
London Business School

INTRODUCTION

If you read no further than this page, we want you to know two things before you put the book down:

1. Millennials want to be happy and effective at work.
2. You can provide an environment where Millennials can be both happy and effective without ruining your organization, if you focus on what actually is important to them.

These two points are the essence of what we'll be talking about. But the trick is knowing what to do. In this book, you'll learn who Millennials are, what they want, and what to *do about it*.

"But it's impossible to make Millennials happy," you might say. "They are so unreasonable! They want the newest gadgets. They want to work three-hour days at full pay and to bring their pet, or their parents, or both to work every day. They don't understand how business works! If you knew about the bizarre things I've seen them do or heard the stories I've heard, you wouldn't say that it is possible to make them happy without changing the very nature of work!"

Well, sometimes appearances—and even behavior—can be misleading. We'll explain how Millennials view the world of work, what they want, and how you can deal with them effectively, whether you are a coworker, a manager, an HR professional, or someone in charge of talent strategy for your organization.

Fundamentally, Millennials want to do interesting work with people they enjoy, for which they are well paid, and still have enough time to live their lives as well as work. Everything you need to do about Millennials follows from there.

Let's Start with Who We Are Calling Millennials

Throughout the book we use "Millennials" to refer to a specific group of people, those born between 1980 and 2000. They have also been called Echo Boomers, Gen Y, and NetGen.

Millennials have grown up with greater access to technology than earlier generations. They are typically proficient with new technology (some say addicted to technology and uninterested in human contact), and many people believe their skill with new technology makes Millennials an asset to organizations.

Millennials have also been described as needy and entitled. Their detractors say that is because life was easy for them when they were growing up, at least in comparison with their parents. On the other hand, many of their families experienced financial hardship as a result of economic and social shifts. So some people posit that these hardships make Millennials skeptical of organizations in general and authority within organizations in particular. They have been derided as disloyal, uncommitted, and unwilling to work hard.

We have found these stereotypes of Millennials to be largely the same everywhere we have done our research. Though the details of the behaviors associated with these stereotypes might differ, the basics are consistent in all of the countries included in our research.

How We Got Here

This book introduces and explains the results of a series of projects we have worked on between 2008 and 2015. The data used for this book are global and include a total of more than 25,000 responses from Millennials and more than 29,000 responses from older employees from 22 countries. The research included both surveys and fieldwork conducted by us (Jennifer and Alec) and our colleagues directly with global organizations, and from the World Leadership Survey, which is an ongoing research effort funded by the Center for Creative Leadership. In addition to these data, we conducted numerous interviews and focus group meetings in most of the countries. The work of many of our colleagues helped produce the data used here, and we are grateful to them for their contributions.

We decided to write this book because we hear so many generalizations about Millennials promoted by pundits, consultants, and even some researchers—generalizations based mostly on anecdotes and not on real and rigorous data. Just as important, even when the conclusions reached by others are based on data, they typically focus on only one or two factors, not the complete package of who Millennials are and what they want.

When we took a step back to think about what we had learned from all of our different projects, we realized that we had developed an unexpectedly complex picture of Millennials globally. Considering all of the stereotypes we had read about in newspapers and online and had heard about from clients and colleagues alike, we kept finding ourselves saying "yes, but . . ." or "no, but . . ." The caricature-like descriptions we heard didn't live up to the complex reality we encountered during interviews and focus groups and saw in our data. Since our job (our calling actually, but that's a different conversation) is to provide information that people at all levels in organizations can use to make themselves and their workplaces more effective, we decided it was time for something different from the caricatures of Millennials. Those who work with and lead Millennials need an accurate picture of what the Millennials want from work, and how organizations can benefit from that knowledge: a picture that is both nuanced and simple enough to be actionable.

So that's what we intend to do. But before we start, some background information.

Who We Studied

The survey data reported in this book come from just under 25,000 Millennial respondents from 22 countries: Brazil, Canada, China, the Czech Republic, France, Germany, India, Italy, Japan, Korea, Mexico, the Netherlands, Poland, Russia, Singapore,

South Africa, Spain, Switzerland, Taiwan, the United Kingdom, the United Arab Emirates, and the United States. Those respondents work in more than 300 different organizations, most medium to large in size. All sectors of the economy are represented in the data set: government, non-profit, and for-profit. Industries include technology, food service, retail, aerospace, manufacturing, and professional services, among others. The majority of our survey data comes from organizations in the professional services industry, which is also where we conducted most of the interviews and focus groups. While our data are global, the majority of survey responses are from the United States.

Because we find it to be impossible to talk about Millennials without mentioning other generations, we periodically include data from more than 29,000 people from older generations in our databases (primarily Gen Xers and Baby Boomers). These older respondents come from the same organizations and industries as the Millennials we are studying.

While the standard definition of the Millennial generation encompasses everyone on the planet born in a 20-year range, we studied only those Millennials currently in the workforce, which means those born from 1980 to 1995. Most stereotypes about the Millennial generation at work primarily focus on a specific subset: people in professional, technical, managerial, and executive positions who have college degrees (bachelor's or higher). Our sample reflects this, so it is made up of Millennials in these types of positions. Our sample doesn't represent all Millennials everywhere.

In general, we find that Millennials around the globe have remarkably similar perceptions about the workplace. Differences show up in how strongly people respond to a certain topic, not the direction of the belief. And the differences are largely a function of individuals' economic environments. For example, all Millennials keep an eye out for new opportunities, and well-educated Millennials in developing economies (e.g., Brazil, India, and China) often have more opportunities to change jobs than those in economies which are more mature (e.g., France). Where we see interesting country differences in the global data, we make note of it.

Organizational Level

All of the participants included in the results reported here were in support, professional, managerial, and executive roles (for more detailed information by country, see Appendix I.1).

TABLE I.1 Millennials and Organizational Level

Administrative/Nonprofessional	6%
Professional	44%
First-level Manager	34%
Mid-level Manager	14%
Director/Executive	2%

Gender

The sample was well balanced with regard to gender, including slightly more men than women (51 percent men, 49 percent women; for more detailed information by country, see Appendix I.2). Though Millennial men's and women's responses to some of the questions did differ slightly in some countries, the differences weren't large. We will tell you when the differences are meaningful.

Education

Most respondents in all countries and at all levels had university degrees (80 percent). In some cases, people were working at a job while simultaneously pursuing a university degree.

Married and Children

Although they are young, 25 percent were married, and 9 percent had children. Twenty percent of those who had children said they had primary childcare responsibilities (for more detailed information by country, see Appendix I.3).

As noted earlier, our sample is not representative of all Millennials everywhere. We are not claiming it is. It is, however, a very large sample of Millennials working in a range of organizations in professional or quasi-professional roles. This book speaks to the characteristics, behaviors, proclivities, and desires of that group.

Generalizations Are Not Always True—Including This One

Now that you know how we collected the data used for this book, it is important to explain that no matter how many people you survey and interview, and no matter how complex and apparently accurate your statistics are, there will always be some who don't fit the general descriptions. In other words, *no generalizations about people are always true, including the ones in this book.*

Why? Because there are always outliers—people who don't fit a generalization. For example, in general men are taller than women. But every man isn't taller than every woman. In fact, some women are taller than most men. So while the generalization that men are typically taller than women is true, it isn't true for every man and every woman.

Even though there are outliers, that doesn't mean the generalizations are wrong. It just means that any generalization that claims that it is always correct for everyone everywhere is . . . wrong. One of us currently has a late Millennial (teenage) daughter who fits many of the generalizations of a technology-obsessed young person who communicates with her friends only through social media and texting—except that she prefers to read books on paper. So even when a generalization is usually correct, it can be off the mark on occasion.

One of the issues with social science research is that we can't make claims with as much precision as physical scientists, such as chemists and physicists. While chemicals consistently have the same reactions with other chemicals, and apples on Earth always fall down rather than up, people are not so well behaved. Practically, that means that while we have great confidence in the accuracy of what we are saying, there will always be people who are exceptions to the general rule; there are always going to be some men who are shorter than most women, and some women who are taller than most men. To make sure people understand that the general rules aren't true all of the time, many people automatically add qualifiers (what we call "weasel words"). These are words that make sure the reader doesn't think that the authors are asserting that what they are saying is true for everyone everywhere in every circumstance forever and ever—words such as "sometimes," "can be," "may be," and so on.

We are going to make a lot of generalizations in this book. These generalizations are backed up by data and will be accurate for most cases, though not necessarily all. But we don't like weasel-words. So rather than inserting qualifiers in most sentences (which would make this book just as tedious to read as it would be to write), we ask that every time you see us making an assertion or generalization, you should remember that we are also saying the following:

This is true for many—we believe most—Millennials,
under many—we believe most—circumstances,
but isn't true for all Millennials everywhere in every circumstance.
And just because we can all think of a Millennial
who doesn't fit this description perfectly,
that doesn't invalidate the general principle.

While the generalizations are generally applicable to Millennials, there isn't one universal solution for how you address any one Millennial in every single context. In most cases, the insights and advice are applicable regardless of how you interact with Millennials—understanding them is fundamental to interacting with them effectively, whatever your level. However, each recommendation isn't universally applicable, so we have sections with specific recommendations for working with Millennials and for managing Millennials. The information is general. How you apply it is specific.

Much of What Is True About Millennials also Holds for Gen Xers and Baby Boomers

If you're a member of the Millennial generation reading this book, we hope your response in many instances will be, "Yes! That's so true. They get us!" And if you're a member of an older generation, we expect your response in many cases will be, "Why are you saying this is just their generation? We asked for these things years ago! That's what we said! That's what we want, too!"

In reality, a lot of what makes people tick doesn't change from one generation to the next. In our research on Millennials, we discovered many interesting characteristics that make this generation unique. But we also found that in most ways, Millennials' expectations about work are strikingly similar to those of other generations. In many cases, Millennials are continuing a decades-long tradition of pushing organizations to change. We provide information about what Millennials want from work because the purpose of this book is to describe who Millennials are. While we occasionally compare Millennials and older staff where we think the contrasts or similarities are particularly interesting, an exhaustive comparison is beyond the scope of this book. However, we believe the majority of the recommendations we make for managers will be as effective for Gen Xers and Baby Boomers as they are for Millennials.

If we're all the same, why bother to think about one generation at all, you might ask? Change is incremental, and what seemed like a massive shift when it was begun by Baby Boomers or Gen Xers can look like no big deal to someone who walks into the workplace with the change firmly in place. The benefit of a new generation entering the working world is that its members look at the workplace with a lens unclouded by past experience with the organization. When members of a new generation start working with us, their presence and new perspective can help shake us out of complacency, making us question some of the fundamental assumptions about why we do things the way we do. That's a good thing.

A Brief Thank-You

While our names are on the front of the book, we wrote it with considerable assistance from a lot of people; we hope we thanked all of them in the acknowledgments. The work of many of our colleagues helped produce the data used here, and we are grateful to them for their contributions. It is incredible to us how many people were kind enough to give up their scarce free time to be interviewed, comment, help, read, review, and kibitz, rather than do something that was personally important to them. It is a gift for which we cannot thank them enough. So if you like what you find in the book, be sure to thank them because they helped make it that way. For anything you don't like, complain to us!

One Last Thing Before You Start Reading

This book presents five core chapters that address stereotypes of Millennials we have found consistently around the world and two chapters about the implications for now (Chapter 6) and for the future (Chapter 7).

Our research revealed that, fundamentally, Millennials want what older generations have always wanted: an interesting job that pays well, where they work with people they like and trust, have access to development and the opportunity to advance, are shown appreciation on a regular basis, and don't have to leave. They are focused on three key areas: the people, the work, and the opportunities. Hopefully, the knowledge gained from the research will help all of us bring their (and really, everyone's) desires closer to being realized. Even if you follow our advice, we can't promise that all issues with Millennials will miraculously disappear and you will have nirvana at work. However, we are confident that your organization will be a much better place in which to work, and the Millennials will be more engaged with their work and teams and more committed to the organization overall.

CHAPTER 1

ENTITLED *AND* HARDWORKING

Carl is an engineer in a large technology firm. He's part of a small team that's on a tight deadline to finish a component for a larger system that will make his organization billions of dollars. Like the rest of his team, Carl works long hours, often staying until 8 p.m. in the clean lab, testing options and working to optimize the component ahead of the deadline.

While his boss thinks Carl is a good, hardworking engineer, he also thinks Carl acts entitled because he frequently arrives after 11 a.m., with just enough time to turn on his computer and find out what his team is working on before he goes to lunch with his friends. Carl told his boss that he works late, so he should be able to come in late—every day he had worked late the night before. He pointed out that no one had been asking for his help earlier in the morning, so why was there a need for him to be there? The boss disagreed, as did the rest of the team, all of whom left equally late and still managed to arrive by 9 a.m.

Carl didn't see a need to change his behavior, so his boss decided to create a reason for him to be there and started having a standing morning meeting at 9:15 a.m. to go over the team's goals for the day with the team. Carl missed the first one, arriving just before 11 a.m. His boss talked with him, telling him it was important to be at the meeting. He missed the second one, arriving just after 10 a.m. Again, his boss talked with him. Finally, Carl made the third meeting— and all of the rest of them until the project was done. While Carl was unwilling to come in to work at a particular time just because his boss wanted him to, when there was a compelling reason, such as a team meeting, he was quite happy to come in at the earlier time. And he did work hard. The component the team was responsible for was finished with better specifications than had been planned on the original timeline.

MILLENNIALS ARE ENTITLED, RIGHT?

We're sure most people have heard the complaint that Millennials act entitled. That is certainly what Carl's boss thinks. He thinks Carl needs to grow up and understand that other people are working long hours as well and that he should arrive at the office at a reasonable time, which isn't right before lunch. Carl is what many see as a stereotypical Millennial employee—wanting to do what he wants to do when he wants to do it and unconcerned about workplace expectations, such as when he arrives at work. At the same time, he worked very hard, contributed to the project, and was willing to change his behavior when it was necessary to get the work done.

Millennials have been characterized as demanding the best of everything. If they aren't interested in the work, they don't want to do it. They feel they can say anything to anyone at work, regardless of that person's position within the organization. They believe they should have work-life balance from their first day on the job, rather than earning the right to it.

i don't have a problem with entitlement! the problem is that i'm not getting everything i want!

Toothpaste for Dinner.com

Many of the complaints about Millennials' sense of entitlement are focused in three areas:

- They want a life outside of work.
- They think they can say whatever they like.
- They don't want to do repetitive work.

Having heard these complaints from clients around the world, we investigated. What we have found is considerably more interesting—and useful—than the stereotype.

Millennials Are Entitled . . . They Want a Life Outside of Work

A common reason Millennials are called entitled is because they want to have a fulfilling life in addition to work, and they want it now rather than some time in the future. They want to have a good job that is interesting and pays well, but they do not want to sacrifice their quality of life to achieve it. They are continuing the tradition of employees pushing organizations so that they can achieve a better life for themselves and their families.

It is true that Millennials want to have enough time to enjoy their lives outside of work. And they don't feel they have it. We find that more than half of Millennials say that their work often interferes with their personal lives in a way that makes it difficult to fulfill their personal responsibilities.

- 63 percent of Millennials say that work demands interfere with their home and personal life.
- 59 percent say that the amount of time their job takes makes it difficult for them to fulfill their personal responsibilities.
- 68 percent say that they have had to change their personal plans because of work.

Yes, Work-Life Balance Does Differ by Country, but . . .

The percentage of Millennials reporting problems with having enough time for life outside of work varies quite a bit across the different countries in our dataset (see Figure 1.1).

The tension that people feel between work and home life is created by multiple factors, including societal norms, each individual's circumstances and career preferences, as well as the volume of work. Working long hours is a cause of work-life balance problems, but how the long hours are experienced depends quite a bit on the individual and the expectations of the job. We find that within every country there is a big difference between people in executive, managerial, and professional positions—high-responsibility, high-stress jobs—and those in administrative support roles.

People often make sweeping statements about differences across countries with regard to how hardworking the citizens are. Yet how many hours someone in a particular role works is remarkably similar across countries. Across the globe, people who work in high-responsibility, high-workload, high-stress jobs tend to report more work-life issues than people in lower-level,

FIGURE 1.1: Percentage of Millennials Who Indicated That the Demands of Work Interfere with Their Home and Personal Life vs. Average Hours Worked per Week (for those working full-time)

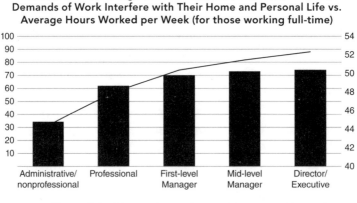

■■■ % agree (left axis)   ——— Average hours worked per week (right axis)

support-type jobs. The job you are in matters as much or even more than the country you do it in.

———————————————————————————

Part of the reason Millennials are so concerned about having enough time for their lives away from work is that they feel like they're never off the clock. The prevalence of smartphones and other devices means that employees can be contacted about work at any time—and often are. During our interviews, we found that Millennials usually don't mind work interrupting their personal time, but if work is going to continue after hours, they expect to have enough time away from work demands so they don't have to postpone enjoying their lives now.

One Millennial we spoke with talked about how frustrated he was because he worked so many hours. He wasn't frustrated because he had children or a spouse he felt he was neglecting, or even a serious romantic relationship. He was frustrated because work interfered with his personal activities, such as going to see his nephews and nieces in their school performances and sporting events or playing on his rugby team. Having time to pursue personal interests is important to everyone, not just those with immediate family obligations.

Millennials are willing to and do work long hours, but they don't believe that spending a lot of time in the office indicates they are working hard. Only 1 in 20 believes that how long people spend in the office reflects how productive they are. They view that attitude as an anachronism, a holdover from an era when the "company man" dedicated his life to work and everyone aspired to that norm.

Millennial men and women don't differ in their perspectives on this—neither group believes that spending a lot of time in the office indicates that they are working hard or are productive. However, the Millennials who work the longest hours (more than 50 per week) are slightly more likely to believe that spending a lot of time in the office shows they are working hard.

We think this difference is driven partly by how some people get work done. While not all work has to happen in the office, many people feel they get more done when they're working physically near colleagues on their team. They think that because they themselves are more productive when working in the same place as their colleagues, if others are working at home (or anywhere else), they are not as productive. Also, people who work a lot of hours may not believe that everyone else is working as hard as they are if they can't see them. This sentiment, held by particularly hardworking Millennials, is similar to that of many managers who don't believe people are working hard if they are out of the office.

But not all managers feel this way. More than two-thirds of Millennials say that their individual manager is accommodating of their personal lives and allows flexible schedules. During an interview, one manager of Millennials spoke at length about the importance of flexibility at work, both for her employees and herself. She was quite open about how important work-life balance was to her and how she used her flexible work arrangements to achieve that balance. She was willing to take calls and do work whenever necessary, regardless of the time of day, so she could be where she needed to be for her children and husband. In fact, she said she couldn't have continued to work without the flexibility. As a result of her experience, she made sure the Millennials on her team also had the flexibility they needed to meet their obligations at home.

A particularly telling point emerged during our interview with her. She said that she probably worked more hours overall as a result of the flexibility she was allowed, but she didn't mind at all because it meant everyone's needs were met. Despite the additional hours, she felt that she could meet most of her work and her personal obligations most of the time, so she didn't have to worry. That lack of worry was priceless to her, and she wanted her Millennial employees to have that feeling as well.

Millennials do want a life outside of work. But they are also willing to have that life interrupted by work during nonwork hours when necessary.

Face Time vs. Flexibility

Millennials believe in the importance of flexibility and don't think it is necessary to spend every waking hour in the office. However, they also recognize that traditionally, face time was required at work because employers did not trust their employees to put in enough time or effort. Millennials know that their managers often "grew up" at work with much less flexibility than current technology allows. What many don't understand is why managers today still want to be able to watch their employees all the time. Millennials expect managers to focus on whether their teams perform well and get their work done on time, not *where* or *when* they do their work.

This can become an issue for Millennials, bosses, and organizations in two ways. First, employee evaluations are based both on employees' output and their soft skills (their ability to get along with others, influence, and political savvy, among others). It is difficult to assess soft skills at a distance. So even though working outside the office may be productive, it doesn't always provide enough interaction for the boss to be able to evaluate an employee's soft skills. Second, when Millennials spend a lot of time out of the office or doing distance work, it may limit their opportunities to practice and demonstrate the soft skills necessary to succeed in organizations. This is an issue for anyone who wants to move up, because the higher you go in an organization, the more critical these skills are for success. Therefore, while flexibility is necessary, it is also important that bosses make clear to Millennials how the other aspects of their work will be evaluated. Millennials need to understand the trade-offs for their own development and careers inherent in extreme flexibility.

The Point

Millennials are willing to work long hours and to be contacted outside of working hours when it is necessary to get the job done. At the same time, they want enough time to pursue their personal interests. Managers who capitalize on employees' willingness to be contacted outside of normal work hours need to ensure that the employees still have enough time to pursue their personal interests and don't feel taken advantage of. One way to do that is to allow a flexible schedule as much as possible. If flexible schedules are allowed, managers need to establish clear expectations regarding work output, quality, and timelines.

Millennials Fear Using Work-Life Balance Programs

While work-life balance is important to Millennials, many Millennials believe that organizations and managers are not supportive of it. About a third of Millennials don't think they can make use of organizationally sponsored work-life programs or make choices that are in their best interest without substantial negative repercussions for their careers. Specifically,

- 32 percent believe that if they participate in work-life programs they will be perceived as less dedicated than those who do not.
- 32 percent believe that those who do use work-life programs are less likely to advance their careers.

Millennials Are Entitled . . . They Think They Can Say What They Want

One of the attributes of Millennials that causes people to call them entitled is their apparent belief that they should be able to say what they want. For example, we were told about a 24-year-old intern working in a medium-sized organization. He was a very hard worker, and his supervisor was quite pleased with his performance for the first half of the internship. Then something changed. About halfway through the internship, he would refuse when the supervisor asked him to do something. After this had happened a few times, the supervisor asked him why he was refusing to do the work. He replied, "The first half of the internship was supposed to be about how I could help you. The second half is supposed to be about you helping me. So I'm not going to do any work that isn't focused on helping me. I need to find what interests me, and I'm going to do only work that helps me do that."

Examples like this imply that Millennials believe they can say anything to anyone under any circumstance, including being critical of supervisors, either implicitly (as in the example above) or explicitly. To many, a willingness to be critical of supervisors indicates a lack of deference to hierarchies and people in power. To others, it indicates that Millennials are continuing the tradition of breaking down barriers. Many people at higher levels have told us that they never would have spoken to their bosses the way Millennials speak to them. Perhaps they wouldn't have. But don't we all want to be able to say what we want to say? There has been a cultural change in the past 30 years in how acceptable it is for people lower in the hierarchy to express opinions directly to people higher up, and that includes younger people expressing their opinions to older people.

There are likely multiple sources of this cultural change. Society in general is less formal today than it was a generation ago. People are much less likely to use formal titles when addressing each other. Within organizations there is a more open communication environment, fostered by encouraging lower-level employees to speak up, make contributions, and point out problems to improve the business, regardless of their age or tenure with the organization.

Millennials reflect this cultural shift, with a strong majority believing employees should be able to disagree with their supervisor, even about something as sensitive as a performance appraisal. Millennials also believe that they should be able to be critical of their supervisor. This really is a general cultural shift; similar percentages of Gen Xers and Baby Boomers also feel that way. In fact:

- 91 percent of Millennials (and 94 percent of everyone else) think that employees should feel free to discuss their opinions with their supervisor when their performance appraisal doesn't fit with what they think it should be.

- 64 percent of Millennials (and 61 percent of everyone else) think it is acceptable for young people to be critical of their supervisors.

This cultural shift holds true across countries for Millennials (see Figure 1.2), and for those employees older than Millennials as well (see Appendix 1.1). In all countries, more than 60 percent of Millennials are willing to at least discuss their performance appraisal if it didn't meet their expectations. The countries with the lowest percentage of agreement among Millennials (still over 60 percent agreement) are those where people traditionally are more likely to defer to authority and where acting in a manner that could be perceived as challenging the boss is unacceptable, such as Korea and China. In a large portion of the countries, more than 90 percent of Millennial respondents said they would discuss their performance appraisal with their boss if it didn't meet their expectations.

Yet that willingness to take the initiative to discuss the performance appraisal should not be mistaken for a more general willingness to be confrontational, as can be seen in Figure 1.3. When it comes to being critical of supervisors, the numbers are much smaller. Overall, 64 percent of Millennials believe it is acceptable to be critical of supervisors, and in most countries more than half of Millennials believe this is acceptable.

Though the stereotype is that Millennials in the United States are especially likely to be critical, only 73 percent of U.S. Millennials believe it is acceptable, which is substantially lower than the percentage for Millennials in the Netherlands, of whom 95 percent believe it is acceptable. Spain is the country (in our data) where the smallest percentage of Millennials believe it is acceptable to be critical of supervisors.

People who are older than Millennials are just as likely as Millennials to say it is acceptable to criticize supervisors. Only in Singapore, the United Kingdom, Canada, France, the United States, and South Africa are older employees substantially less

FIGURE 1.2: Percentage of Millennials Who Will Discuss Their Performance Appraisal with Their Supervisor If It Doesn't Meet Their Expectations

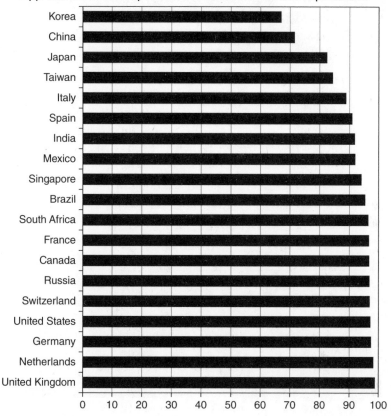

likely than Millennials to say it is acceptable to be critical of supervisors (see Appendix 1.2).

Being willing to criticize supervisors doesn't mean that Millennials want to eliminate hierarchies within organizations. More than three-quarters of Millennials believe that hierarchies are useful.[1] Millennials want to know where and how they can contribute their ideas and actually be heard. Having clear lines of authority helps them identify where it would be best for them to contribute ideas. If you provide clear and sufficient avenues for Millennials to contribute, you will set the stage for a more engaged and productive environment for your Millennial employees—and everyone else.

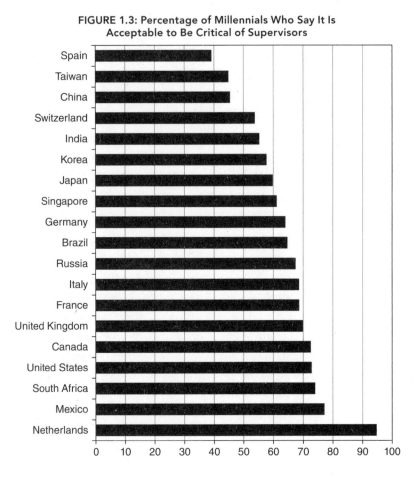

FIGURE 1.3: Percentage of Millennials Who Say It Is Acceptable to Be Critical of Supervisors

Millennials feeling free to speak up makes some people uncomfortable. Some people believe the younger generation has to spend a considerable amount of time with the organization to earn the right to speak up, just as they have to earn flexibility as part of "paying their dues." Managers and organizations benefit, however, when they let go of these attitudes and instead base expectations on what enables productive and engaging work for all employees.

The Point

Millennials believe they should have a say, regardless of their level in or tenure with the organization. Employees are more engaged with work when they are encouraged to contribute their ideas. These contributions are more useful when managers help employees learn how, where, and when to speak up. When they do this, managers both encourage employees to contribute and reduce the amount of time spent dealing with unsolicited recommendations.

Millennials Are Entitled . . . They Don't Like Repetitive Work

When we hear people talk about Millennials being entitled, one of the common complaints is that they dislike doing work they find uninteresting. (Doesn't everyone, you ask? The short answer is yes. More later.) Some point to Millennials who refuse to do the work; others talk about Millennials who will do the work but complain about it.

The truth is that some Millennials think the work they are doing is routine and doesn't have enough variety. Yet the majority of Millennials do *not* feel that way about their jobs; less than a quarter complained about having too much routine work. The data clearly show that a majority of Millennials do not feel that their jobs are without variety. In fact:

- 76 percent did not say their job was routine
- 80 percent thought their job had enough variety

While the majority of Millennials didn't say that their job was too routine, 20 to 25 percent of Millennials *do* believe that their jobs are too routine and don't have enough variety. This isn't positive, either for the Millennials in those jobs or for the organizations that employ them: having too much routine work is related to lower commitment and lower retention. But the data show this is not simply a characteristic of Millennials. Nearly as many older staff believe that their job is routine (18 percent) or doesn't have enough variety (15 percent).

Toothpaste for Dinner.com

If being born Millennials does not cause people to think that their jobs are boring, what is the root cause? Our data suggest that level within the organization is the root cause. The higher you are in the organization, the less routine and lacking in variety your work is, regardless of your generation (see Figures 1.4 and 1.5). This is consistent with the evidence that people at higher levels in an organization—who have greater autonomy—find their work to be more interesting.[2,3,4] That's not a surprise, because lower-level jobs are known to be less interesting and have less variety than those higher in the organization.

For example, in one interview, we heard Millennials talk about how unnecessary some of the work they were doing was and how frustrating they found it. They would e-mail their work to their boss, who would print it out, make (often close to illegible) notes on the paper, and then hand it back to them. It was the Millennials' job to make the corrections that were included in the notations—and then send the revised document back to the boss for another round of edits. What the Millennials found frustrating was the boss's willingness to make the Millennials do unnecessary and boring work (typing in changes multiple times), when all the boss had to do was make notes in the document itself by using the "track changes" function. They thought it could be done much more efficiently.

FIGURE 1.4: My Job Is Routine

■ Millennials: % agree my job is routine ☐ Older Staff: % agree my job is routine

FIGURE 1.5: My Job Does Not Have Enough Variety

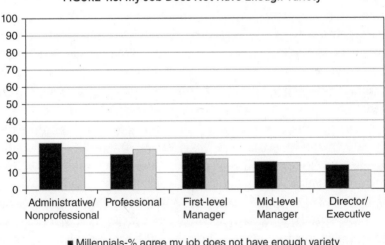

■ Millennials-% agree my job does not have enough variety
☐ Older Staff-% agree my job does not have enough variety

The Millennials we spoke with who had this complaint—on four different continents—understood that the changes had to be made and that they should be the ones to make them. They knew that their time was less valuable than their bosses' and that there was value in them making the changes because they could learn from the experience. What they couldn't understand was why the whole process had to be so laborious. It would have been much more efficient if the boss had simply typed in the changes or written notes using the "comment" function so the Millennials could make the changes themselves rather than writing notes on paper. That approach would have prevented all the issues with illegible handwriting, multiple checks for mistakes, and so on. In this case, the Millennials were unmotivated to do the work not just because it was boring but also because so much of it was unnecessary.

Since Millennials are younger, they are more likely to be in lower-level jobs in the organization. The fact that Millennials in higher-level jobs are less likely than those in lower-levels jobs to say that their work is repetitive is additional evidence for our point: thinking work is boring is not just a characteristic of Millennials; it is a characteristic of the work itself. The interesting question is why Millennials in particular have a bad reputation for complaining about uninteresting work. After all, how many people are motivated when their work is boring and repetitive? We all have work we have to do that we don't want to do for one reason or another. And people frequently complain about the work they don't like. How is it different when Millennials do the complaining?

One aspect that *is* different is that Millennials are younger than many of their colleagues, and people generally believe that young people need to "pay their dues." In many cases, this translates into "do what you're told to do, no matter how boring, repetitive, or routine, without complaining about it. Also, you should be grateful to have the boring, repetitive, and routine work because you don't know much and we're taking you on and teaching you what to do." Or something along those lines. To many in charge, a key part of employees paying their dues means not complaining about the boring work—and Millennials disagree with that.

The Point

While Millennials may object to boring work, they understand that everyone has to do some of it. Routine, repetitive, and boring work becomes an issue when there is more of it than is reasonable, or when it could easily be avoided. Managers should work with their teams and organization to figure out how to reduce the amount of boring and repetitive work where possible, possibly by implementing new approaches or trying new technologies. Managers should also work to increase the variety in day-to-day activities to reduce the burden of routine work. In addition, they should take the time to explain why the tasks are necessary and how they fit into the goals of the team and the organization. Often, work will seem less boring if employees understand how it contributes to the larger mission.

Millennials Are Entitled (and so Is Everyone Else)

Perhaps Millennials are entitled. More than 40 percent of Millennials say they demand the best because they are worth it, believe that they deserve more things in their life, and believe that they deserve an extra break now and then. At the same time, the majority of Millennials don't believe that they deserve special treatment or that things should go their way.

But Millennials aren't the only ones who are entitled. In fact, *about the same percentage* of those older than Millennials also say they demand the best because they are worth it, believe that they deserve more things in their life, believe that they deserve an extra break now and then, and don't believe that they deserve special treatment or that things should go their way.

So Millennials are entitled—just as their role models are.

The data indicate that many of the behaviors that result in Millennials being considered entitled actually come from their strong work ethic and desire to contribute. Managers need to recognize and accept that the attitudes many believe make Millennials entitled are common among employees of all ages and at all levels of an organization. Rather than being concerned about these ubiquitous attitudes, managers need to focus on being clear about their expectations for productivity and communication. When there is conflict, managers should make sure that everyone is clear on what the expectations are.

Entitled Doesn't Mean Lazy

Millennials may hold some expectations that cause people to accuse them of being entitled, but that doesn't mean they are lazy. In fact, we find that Millennials as a group work very hard, are quite motivated, and really want to contribute to their organizations.

One area where this is especially apparent is in Millennials' desire to learn and develop on the job. A study by Universum found that 39 percent wanted to learn new things on a daily basis, and 45 percent said they would spend time to learn new things if given the opportunity to prioritize[5].

In our interviews and focus groups it was clear that employees around the world expect developmental opportunities and coaching at work because their learning will benefit their employer. They also believe that continuous improvement is necessary for their long-term success. While they may feel entitled to learning and developmental opportunities, they are also willing to dedicate a great deal of their own time to learning and often do so, in addition to working long hours.

Millennials Are Hardworking . . . They Work Long Hours

We found that Millennials in our study work really hard: 56 percent work more than 9 hours a day, and 33 percent work more than 10 hours a day (the same is true for those older than Millennials). We were told stories about Millennials working so many hours that they used their homes as large closets—basically going home to shower, maybe sleep for a couple of hours, and change clothes before going straight back to work. Many Millennials talked about regularly working past 11 p.m. in the office when they were on deadlines or their organizations were experiencing particularly busy periods.

The primary reason most work these hours is that their workloads are heavier than what they can possibly get done in a normal work day. As a result, a large percentage of Millennials feel over-loaded at work:

- 42 percent say they can't get everything done on their job.
- 36 percent don't think the amount of work they're being asked to do is reasonable.
- 27 percent believe that because of the workload, they cannot possibly do their work well.

While these were all Millennials in professional, managerial, and executive roles, they weren't all in the technology industry, which has a reputation for Millennials practically living in the office; these included Millennials in consulting, law, banking, consumer goods, and medicine as well.

Work for Millennials doesn't end when they leave the office. Ninety-one percent say they are contacted outside of work hours: 67 percent at least once a week, 12 percent every day. Four out of five Millennials[6] say they read work-related e-mails on their smartphones, and more than a third[7] do so on smartphones they pay for themselves. Millennials who are higher in the organization were more likely to be contacted outside of work hours, with a quarter[8] of those at the highest level reporting that they were contacted every day. So regardless of how many hours Millennials have worked in the office, they do more when they get home. Millennials don't expect work to stop when they leave the office. They have come of age at a time when the mobile workplace is a reality and there is no real "off" time.

Millennials work many hours, are contacted frequently outside of work hours about work issues, and feel overloaded with work. When they express frustration about not having enough personal time to pursue their interests, it's because they have very heavy workloads. They have real trouble finding enough time in the day to get their work done and still have a life. After decades of organizations figuring out how to squeeze ever greater productivity out of their existing workforce (to avoid increasing headcount), employees' reaction to the current design of work is hardly surprising.

The Point

Like older employees at every level, Millennials are overloaded. They are willing to work long hours, but over time become less engaged and more resentful if they don't have enough time for their personal lives. Overworking employees results in more errors, lower engagement, and increased turnover. Organizations need to consider whether being understaffed with overloaded employees is good for business in the long term.

Millennials Are Hardworking . . . Because They Are Strongly Motivated

We find that Millennials are highly intrinsically motivated and are very motivated by the type of work they do. More than half of Millennials said they were motivated to do their job because it would help them fulfill their career plans[9] or because they enjoyed it.[10] For example, we spoke with one Millennial who couldn't say enough positive things about his work. He had been on the job for about two years, and he spent almost our whole time with him talking about how much he loved his work. He felt he was learning something new almost every day. He felt he was contributing to the team in a meaningful way. And he believed that the work he was doing (even the repetitive work) was helping him fulfill his career plans. He was motivated by the learning opportunities that made the work interesting to him, and by how the work was contributing to his long-term career plans.

While most of the Millennials we spoke with were motivated and excited about the work they were doing and what they were learning, we also found a number who were not. In many cases, these Millennials were doing work they had done for years. They kept getting promoted and paid more because they were doing work the organization appreciated, but they weren't particularly motivated because they no longer felt that they were learning and developing new skills that would help them fulfill their long-term career plans.

Paying more or giving more senior titles to Millennials won't motivate them, because they are motivated less by how much they make and how they are perceived by others than they are by the work itself. (Not that they are unmotivated by those things.) For example, less than a third[11] of Millennials said they were motivated to do their job because it allowed them to make a lot of money.

Though making money isn't the primary motivating factor for most Millennials to do their jobs, don't jump to the mistaken conclusion that money is unimportant. In fact, compensation is *critically* important, as we'll explain in detail in Chapter 3. But compensation isn't necessarily a *motivating* factor. The compensation Millennials receive has to be high enough for them to be willing to take the job, but it doesn't provide motivation by itself for them to do the job to the best of their ability. On the other hand, if the pay is too low, then it is a *demotivating* factor, which we also discuss in Chapter 3, and it can easily drive them to leave. In this way, Millennials are no different from the older generations: pay is extremely important for attraction and retention, but it does little to motivate people to perform at the highest levels.

Overall, the work itself is critically important to Millennials. Being paid a high salary to do uninteresting work won't motivate them, though the level of compensation may keep them around. Millennials want to do work that they find interesting and that they believe will help them with their long-term career plans.

The Point

Millennials are highly intrinsically motivated. That means they are motivated to do work they perceive to be interesting and worthwhile. Work that does not meet those criteria is demotivating. Managers can benefit from their employees' intrinsic motivation. Employees will often go above and beyond their basic job requirements for work they find interesting and believe to be important to their careers.

Do Millennials Care about Spelling, Grammar, and Punctuation?

Many complain that Millennials don't care about writing clearly and provide examples where they said Millennials had sent out documents, e-mails, and presentations that included spelling, grammar, and punctuation errors. The conclusion from this evidence is that Millennials don't care about good grammar and punctuation and use text-speak such as LOL in professional e-mails. Yet 93 percent of Millennials think proper spelling, grammar, and punctuation are important (note: a similar 94 percent of their older coworkers think these are important). Clearly, a majority do care about proper grammar.

Which brings us to the question of whether Millennials are uniquely poor at using correct spelling, grammar, and punctuation or whether the complaints about Millennials represent a larger cultural issue. There have been books written on the premise that Millennials are uneducated and don't care about spelling and punctuation.[12] And there are many examples of documents that have been circulated at organizations that were rife with spelling, punctuation, and grammatical errors. However, in our global interviews, we found that there were complaints of this sort from both older and younger workers about people of all generations.

Older employees complained about Millennials' poor spelling, grammar, and punctuation and occasional use of text-standard acronyms with which they were not familiar, such as CID for *consider it done* or CM for *call me*; in contrast, most people know FYI in place of *for your information*. Similarly, Millennials complained about older employees' apparent inability to use spell-check, thus sending documents with large numbers of errors for Millennials to fix. High-performing

Millennials we spoke with also often complained about the errors they saw in e-mails and documents written by other employees, but they didn't attribute the problem to that employee's generation. Instead, they questioned the individual's competence.

And competence is the real issue. Like anyone else in the workplace, Millennials have to produce good work. On average, Millennials are hardworking, but all new employees need to be told what the expectations are in their new workplace. The more explicit managers can be about their expectations, the more likely it is that the Millennial will meet them. And if managers believe that communications need to use correct grammar, punctuation, and spelling, they should make sure employees understand the importance of that and set the example by doing it themselves.

Millennials Are Hardworking . . . Because They Have a Strong Desire to Contribute

Rather than perceiving themselves as being hired just to do a job, Millennials want to contribute to the organization as much as possible, even beyond the specific requirements of the job. They feel they should be speaking up and sharing their ideas, not only because it benefits them but also because it benefits the organization. And that is how they behave.

For example, Don is a Millennial who works for a large multinational organization. He has been identified as a high potential, someone who is likely to move up into management soon. He is incredibly dedicated, working long hours to make sure the work gets done on time. People in other divisions are very complimentary about how helpful he is to them, often going above and beyond to help them do their jobs.

While his dedication is commendable, sometimes he has difficulty sticking to established hierarchical lines and understanding when it's appropriate to ask for permission instead of forgiveness. For example, one time someone in another group talked with him about an issue, thinking he might have some ideas. He did have some ideas, which he discussed with that person. But he didn't leave it there. He decided he should go to that person's boss to propose a solution—a solution to a problem he was not responsible for and didn't have all of the information about. This annoyed both his boss and the other person's boss—both of whom told him to stop escalating things and do his real job. The issue wasn't that he had commented (his suggestion was a good one) but that he took the issue to higher levels rather than providing his information to the people who were responsible for handling it.

While this incident demonstrates how hardworking Don is, it also shows how a desire to make recommendations that contribute to the organization can be pursued too far and consequently annoy others. Millennials making recommendations isn't uncommon. Three-quarters of Millennials say that they develop and make recommendations to their teams for what to do.[13] A majority of Millennials say that they speak up when they have ideas for new projects or changes in procedures that they believe could help their teams.[14] Since they want to contribute to their teams and organizations, they don't think that they should be quiet simply because they haven't been with the organization as long. Rather, they think they should contribute as much as possible from the moment they join the organization. That attitude sometimes makes older peers and those higher up in the hierarchy uncomfortable. As we mentioned earlier, many believe that employees need to earn the right to speak up, and that they do so by earning credibility, which to many means being older or more advanced in the hierarchy.

While Millennials want to contribute, they realize that others often expect them to follow established protocols for how and when to speak up, and they understand that they may need to be careful about how they contribute. For example, 49 percent believe that disagreeing with a supervisor in front of others is likely to embarrass the supervisor. At the same time,

- 77 percent don't think it is a bad idea to speak up in front of the team without telling the supervisor in advance.
- 73 percent don't believe that they should pass their ideas by supervisors in private first before speaking up in front of the team.

So Millennials want to speak up when they believe they have something constructive to contribute, and they believe they should be able to contribute directly rather than first vetting what they want to say with their supervisors. At the same time, they try to avoid doing things they believe would embarrass their supervisors. Issues likely arise when there are differences in what people perceive as embarrassing. It is quite likely that in some cases, Millennials will not consider something potentially embarrassing that will in fact bother their supervisors.

Extra Work as Contribution

As anyone who has worked knows, there is more to doing a job well than just doing what is in the job description. To perform well, employees take on a myriad of other responsibilities beyond precisely what they were hired to do. One complaint about Millennials is that they are likely to say, "But that's not part of my job," when asked to do something extra. In fact:

- 82 percent volunteer to do things for their teams.
- 88 percent help others on their teams with their responsibilities.
- 78 percent go beyond their job responsibilities to assist others working for their teams.

A majority of Millennials do engage in "extra-role behaviors" like these to help out members of their teams. This is good news because extra-role behaviors are critical to helping an organization function effectively. As people often say, if employees only did what was included in their job descriptions, work would quickly grind to a halt!

The Point

Millennials believe they should be able to say what they think. Though this may make them seem entitled, they are motivated by a strong desire to contribute to their teams and their organizations.

For Millennials, speaking up is not fundamentally about challenging authority. Speaking up is about wanting to make a genuine contribution to organizational processes that need improvement and to have that contribution recognized. Managers can coach Millennials to help them learn how and when it is most effective to speak up.

CONCLUSION: MILLENNIALS ARE BOTH ENTITLED AND HARDWORKING

As you can see, the evidence shows that Millennials are both entitled and hardworking. They work many hours, are willing to be contacted outside of work when necessary, are strongly motivated to do their job, make efforts to contribute beyond their job description, and desire to move up in the organization. At the same time, they don't like to do a lot of boring work, want to have a life outside of work, and expect their workplace to have enough flexibility to allow them to fulfill both their personal and professional commitments. Millennials believe that they have been hired to do a job and that they should speak up if they have something useful to say.

How Different Are Millennials, Really?

"Speak truth to power" is a phrase that has been used since at least the 1950s. So when Millennials tell their bosses what they really think rather than hide it, they are continuing a tradition of speaking up to those who are more powerful. Similarly, older employees want to do interesting work, are motivated to contribute, and want to live balanced lives. As technology makes it easier to work more outside of a physical office, employees of all ages see the advantages that flexibility affords. And they need it: 56 percent of older staff report working more than 9 hours a day, and 33 percent report working more than 10 hours a day, similar to Millennials.

If Millennials and older workers are so similar, why do people perceive them as being so different? The bottom line is that Millennials' behavior is often perceived differently because they

ENTITLED *AND* HARDWORKING   37

are younger and have less organizational tenure, not because they behave differently. Some believe their youth and fewer years of work experience translate to less organizational savvy, less knowledge, and fewer good ideas.

The problem is that we often perceive behavior based on who is doing it. If an older person sends an e-mail that is poorly spelled, people shrug. If Millennials do it, they are viewed as sloppy or not willing to do their job properly. Similarly, if older staff pass off work they don't find interesting while making a comment about having more mission-critical work to do, people understand. When younger people do it, they are seen as not being team players.

Whether Millennials are entitled or just misunderstood, the following sections describe some actions you can take to work with them effectively as a team member, a manager, or a leader.

Recommendations for Working with Millennials as Team Members

While some Millennials may be annoying (some would call them entitled), team members can work effectively with them and benefit from their attitudes. For example, most people don't like boring work any more than Millennials do. But many older people have accepted that it just has to get done—by someone. And it can be quite annoying when Millennials think they are exempt from it.

Though this attitude can be frustrating, you should think about the fact that Millennials are just as frustrated by the boring work as you are. Older teammates might say that they had to do really boring work early in their career, so Millennials should just put up with it as they did. Perhaps they should if there are no other options, but working together you might be able to come up with alternatives that eliminate the repetitive work, or at least reduce it considerably. Millennials may have different ideas or technology options that haven't been explored, and you can use their knowledge and expertise to figure out how the new process could work to reduce the boring work for everyone.

Similarly, though Millennials are willing to work long hours, they also want to have a life outside of work. They understand and agree with your desire to have one, too. Teams that are feeling overburdened can work together to find a solution so everyone isn't working all the time. Perhaps one team member would be happy to come in early, while another would be willing to stay late.

Recommendations for Managing Millennials

1. Minimize repetitive work and engage Millennials to improve processes so everyone's work is more efficient.

While Millennials object to boring work, they recognize that all employees sometimes have to do it. Millennials want to help find other options that will improve the workplace for themselves and everyone else (no one really enjoys doing work he or she finds boring). Employees don't believe that they should keep their heads down and just do what they are told, especially when it is boring and clearly unnecessary. Gone are the days when a manager can bury someone under a mountain of paperwork or really mind-numbing tasks and expect the person to just suck it up. Instead, employees think they should help improve the process so there is less boring work to do for everyone.

Managers are often responsible for distributing work, and they need to monitor the amount of routine work and its effect on employees. Managers should work with their teams to minimize repetitive work and make it less onerous. Where it can't be avoided, take the time to explain why the repetitive work is necessary—how it fits into the larger picture and contributes to your organization's success.

Show employees appreciation for doing this sort of work. In fact, showing appreciation for doing boring work is probably more important than acknowledging when staff accomplish interesting tasks. Succeeding at interesting assignments is intrinsically motivating in and of itself; your appreciation is important but not a primary driver. In the case of boring work, you need both to explain the importance of the work and to show employees that you appreciate them. Otherwise, they will see absolutely no redeeming value in it and are likely to resent you for making them do it.

2. Make use of Millennials' willingness to work long hours, but don't take advantage of them.

Millennials are willing to work hard. Many of them even enjoy putting in long hours when they feel the work is worthwhile, their time is being used effectively, and they are working with people they like (see Chapter 4). If a deadline has to be met, a Millennial employee is just as willing as the next person to put in the necessary time and effort. But their willingness and dedication disappear rapidly when they catch the first whiff of mismanagement. If you use their time inefficiently, if you make them come into the office at odd hours simply to be seen and make them wait for others to engage them, if you bother them at home in the middle of the night or expect them to respond to the most mundane and unimportant queries on e-mail or text during their free time, you will quickly kill their desire to be responsive.

As a manager, you need to find the right balance between workplace demands and employee capacity. When employees complain about work-life balance, they typically do so from a place of dedication and commitment to you, to the work, and to the organization. They are saying, "We are willing to work hard when needed, but don't abuse us." If the demands on their time in the early morning, in the evening, and on weekends are reasonable, employees will likely be willing to do the work. But if you push them too far, they will push back, and rightly so.

3. Encourage employees' desire to contribute ideas, and appreciate their willingness to speak up.

Millennials really want to contribute. They expect to do that not just by correctly executing their job duties; many also want to think beyond their immediate tasks and suggest innovations and ideas that can improve work processes and organizational performance. When you encourage their contributions, it helps show appreciation for their willingness to speak up and their desire to improve the business.

As a manager, you will find Millennials more engaged and excited about the work if you encourage their desire to contribute. Provide them with specific opportunities to contribute and suggestions for areas where their contributions would be helpful and relevant. This will accomplish two important goals. They will be encouraged by the opportunity to contribute. And you will avoid the annoyance of having to fend off their recommendations in areas where their knowledge doesn't match their enthusiasm.

Five Points to Remember

1. Millennials are willing to work long hours.
2. Millennials are strongly motivated to do interesting work, just not repetitive work.
3. Millennials want a life as well as a job.
4. Millennials will speak truth to power.
5. Millennials have a strong desire to contribute.

Who Millennials Are and What They Want

Millennials:
- Want a life outside of work
- Don't mind work interrupting their lives
- Don't think much face time is necessary
- Expect flexibility at work
- Don't like routine work
- Will say what they think to people above them in the hierarchy
- Believe there should be clear lines of authority
- Don't believe they deserve special treatment
- Work long hours
- Are strongly motivated
- Are frustrated by unnecessary work
- Have a strong desire to contribute
- Go out of their way to help team members

CHAPTER 2

NEEDY *AND* INDEPENDENT

Sean, a Millennial, is a first-level manager in a large organization. He's being groomed to move up soon . . . if he can stop tripping himself up. He is an excellent employee. His boss appreciates the fact that he works lots of hours and is always available. He is an independent worker who is motivated to do his job well, clearly wants to contribute, and is willing to take on extra work and go the extra mile to make things happen.

But Sean is perceived as constantly needing affirmation. He frequently asks for feedback about how he's doing and spends a great deal of time publicizing his work within the organization. He has made it clear that he wants to move up and is willing to do what it takes to get there. He wants to know precisely what is necessary to do that and exactly how long it will take.

Sean may be a good worker, but his boss perceives his constant need for affirmation and feedback as needy. Like Sean's boss, many supervisors say that Millennials are needy because they want to know how they're doing all the time. They want to be provided with very specific criteria for success. They want a map to tell them precisely how to get from here to there (with here being their current state and there being nirvana, both personally and professionally), and when they don't get it, they are needy and clingy, wanting constant reassurance. At the same time, they are incredibly independent. They want coaching on how to achieve their goals, but they don't want to be told what to do (which is how they often perceive advice).

Many of the complaints about Millennials being needy are focused in three areas:

- They want their parents involved.
- They want constant mentoring and assistance.
- They want frequent feedback.

Millennials Are Needy, Right?

Millennials are each needy in their own special way. Some have parents who hover; others want bosses to act as parents. Some want to be told every 10 minutes that they are doing well; for others, every half hour or so will do. At least that is what people say. Our data tell a somewhat different story.

Millennials Are Needy . . . They Want Their Parents to Be Involved in Their Work Life

Helicopter parents aren't just for toddlers anymore—they are now well known in the business world.[1] We heard about one high-potential Millennial who failed a drug test for his employer. The Millennial was informed about the results of the test, and a time was set for him to meet with human resources to talk about rehabilitation so he could keep his job. Before that meeting could take place, the Millennial's mother went to his office and demanded that the HR person show her the drug test results, because she didn't believe them. The HR person had to explain that it would be illegal to show her the results of the 27-year-old employee's drug screen, even though he was her child. The mother kept insisting that she had to see the results, because clearly there had been a mistake!

Organizations around the globe have given us similar examples of parents intervening in their adult children's work lives. It was clear to us that attitudes about parental involvement in adult children's lives vary substantially by culture—and often within cultures.

Even opinions regarding asking about parental involvement vary! In the United States and Europe, some considered our questions about parental involvement both inappropriate and unnecessary (why would anyone think parents would be involved, they asked us), although others were pleased that we were considering this issue because they had encountered it many times. People in India, the United States, and China thanked us for bringing up a topic that they struggle with daily!

While some managers have never encountered this before, parental involvement in one form or another is relatively common. Universum's global survey found that a quarter of Millennials surveyed said that they involved their parents in their career decisions,[2] and a 2007 Michigan State University study found that about a third of large companies had witnessed parents being involved in their children's work lives.[3] One area where Millennials' parents are more likely to be involved is the job search and application process. According to the 2007 Michigan State study,[4] 40 percent of respondents said they had observed parents helping their child in the job search process: researching a company, complaining if the company didn't hire their child, actually attending the interview, and so on.

"PLEASE EXCUSE MY MOTHER, THIS IS MY FIRST INTERVIEW."

Source: CartoonStock (www.CartoonStock.com)

We heard similar stories from many organizations. Common stories were about parents appearing in the workplace to negotiate their child's starting salary or to complain that their child had been working too many hours. One manager told us that a parent directly phoned a supervisor to complain about a bad review. Another manager told us about an incident that happened with a new employee:

> *I hired a new employee who was scheduled to start in two weeks. That Monday (his first day at work), he didn't arrive, and no one received a call from him saying where he was. He also didn't appear on Tuesday. On Wednesday, he arrived and presented me with a note saying he had been ill. The note was from his mother.*

The manager didn't think it was appropriate for an adult employee to arrive with a note from his mother excusing his illness. As the manager said to us, this isn't high school, and you don't get an excused absence because your mother says you are ill. He attributed this behavior to Millennials being needy and wanting their parents to continue to take care of them.

While the stories make it sound as if many Millennials want their parents closely involved in their work, we didn't find that to be true. With regard to parental involvement, the issue is really about the *level* of involvement. From what we found and heard during interviews, Millennials want their parents' help but don't want them closely involved. While we heard many stories about parents helping Millennials find their first job, we found that 90 percent of Millennials do not think parents should be involved in their child's job interviews,[5] and 85 percent of Millennials do not think an organization should send parents a copy of their child's offer letter.[6]

Figure 2.1 shows that Millennials in different countries *don't* support parents receiving a copy of their child's offer letter. In most countries, more than 80 percent don't support the idea, though in India, Taiwan, China, Brazil, Korea, and Mexico, it's less than 80 percent. Though few Millennials are clamoring for this type of policy (the vast majority of Millennials in all countries clearly *don't* want parents actively involved in the hiring process), it is interesting

FIGURE 2.1: Percentage of Millennials Who Don't Support
Parents Receiving a Copy of Their Child's Offer Letter

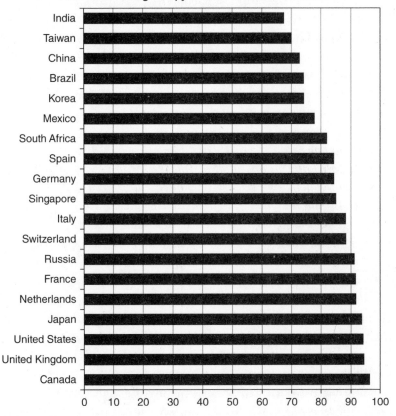

to note the significant minority who want their parents involved: more than 1 in 5 in some of these countries and 1 in 10 in many other countries. Nonetheless, Millennials as a generation clearly are not in favor of parents' actively participating in the hiring process.

Why, then, do people in organizations think most Millennials want their parents involved, when clearly it is a minority in all countries and a very small minority in most countries? This is a good example of how narratives about a generation are created. Someone who knows a few Millennials who want their parents closely involved can easily jump to the conclusion that such views are widespread across the entire generation. Though 10 to 20 percent of the population is a low percentage, it still means that thousands of Millennials want their parents involved. And it doesn't take meeting more than a handful with this perspective for someone to reach the conclusion that most Millennials are like the handful they have met, even if those few are not representative of the generation overall.

Another area we hear complaints about is parents wanting to be involved in the performance review process at their child's first professional job. For example,

> *A college hire who was with us for about nine months was having difficulty getting things done on time. Several coaching sessions were conducted between her and her manager. The manager told her the next time she missed an important deadline, he would have to write her up. When he scheduled a performance management discussion meeting with her, her mom came with her to the meeting. Of course, we told her that her mom couldn't come to the meeting. The mom and the employee were shocked when we told the mom that she needed to leave or wait until the meeting was over to talk to her daughter. They didn't see why the mom couldn't be in the meeting with her daughter.*

While we have heard from managers about parents they've encountered who wanted to know in detail about their children's performance, most Millennials don't want the organization to provide their parents with this information. In fact, 90 percent of Millennials do not support the organization sending parents their child's performance review—let alone having the parents sit in on a performance discussion, as in the prior example.

Millennials may not want their parents to take an active role in their work lives, but a majority of Millennials in all countries, except Japan, discuss their compensation with their parents (see Figure 2.2). In fact, a higher percentage of Millennials discuss their compensation with their parents than with their friends (47 percent) or coworkers (38 percent).[7]

One explanation for this pattern is life stage. We find that Millennials who are single and don't have children are much more likely than those who are married or do have children to discuss

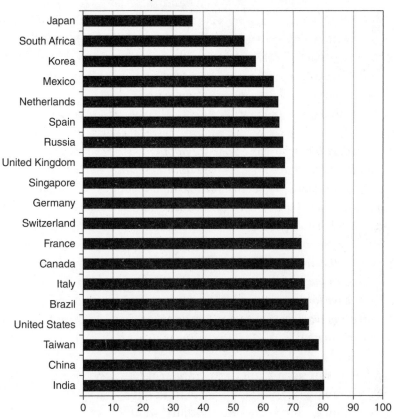

FIGURE 2.2: Percentage of Millennials Who Discuss
Their Compensation with Their Parents

their compensation with their parents (see Table 2.1). Millennials are more likely to discuss their compensation with their parents than are older employees who are in the same life stage. It will be interesting to see if this pattern holds when the Millennials are in their forties, as Gen Xers are now.

TABLE 2.1 Percentage of Employees Who Share Compensation Information with Their Parents

	MARRIED	NOT MARRIED	KIDS	NO KIDS
Millennials	56%	76%	50%	73%
Older Staff	26%	43%	25%	40%

Who Millennials Live With

Part of Millennials' openness in sharing compensation informa-tion with their parents may result from who they are living with. In the United States, there has been an increase in the number of Millennials who live with their parents or with other relatives after having finished university.[8]

Globally, 28 percent of our sample live with their parents; it varies widely based on where the Millennials are from (see Table 2.2). The range across the globe is quite dramatic, from a low of 4 percent in Germany to a high of 67 percent in Sin-gapore. There are many potential factors that cause adult employed children to live with their parents, including their sal-ary and level of debt. But the level of economic development also appears to be a key contributor: countries with higher lev-els of national income are among those with the lowest rates of cohabitation with parents (Germany, France, Switzerland, the United States, the United Kingdom, Canada), while the less developed have among the highest rates (Mexico, India, Brazil, China).

Living with family is common, even expected in some coun-tries, and is done as much for cultural as for economic reasons. For example, we heard from many single Millennials who could afford to live alone but who chose to live with their parents. We heard many Millennials who are married with children talking about how wonderful it is to live with their extended families. (Married Millennials living with their extended family seems particularly common in India.) These are people who have the means to live elsewhere if they wish to, so their choice clearly is a preference rather than an economic necessity.

In addition to culture, the cost of housing is likely a key factor in the choice to continue living with parents. For example, the high population density in Singapore leads to extremely high housing prices, making housing for young people starting off their careers quite expensive. (See Chapter 3 for more discus-sion about housing debt and how it may be affecting Millennials' life and career choices.) Yet economics cannot explain all the

TABLE 2.2 Who Millennials Live With (by Country)

COUNTRY	PARENTS	SPOUSE	CHILDREN	SIBLINGS	OTHER FAMILY	ROOM-MATES	SIGNIFI-CANT OTHER/ PARTNER	ALONE
Brazil	57%	19%	6%	20%	2%	8%	5%	10%
Canada	21%	29%	7%	10%	3%	9%	20%	20%
China	43%	25%	6%	7%	2%	18%	5%	17%
France	6%	47%	10%	3%	1%	6%	17%	26%
Germany	4%	17%	4%	2%	0%	10%	38%	33%
India	59%	35%	10%	18%	5%	13%	1%	9%
Italy	31%	8%	2%	8%	0%	18%	20%	20%
Japan	20%	31%	10%	11%	2%	3%	6%	39%
Korea	50%	22%	8%	27%	2%	1%	0%	20%
Mexico	60%	15%	9%	31%	6%	7%	4%	13%
Netherlands	10%	24%	10%	3%	1%	8%	36%	22%
Russia	26%	33%	12%	6%	1%	11%	16%	16%
Singapore	67%	15%	2%	38%	7%	8%	5%	5%
South Africa	23%	31%	10%	9%	4%	10%	11%	19%
Spain	38%	15%	3%	11%	2%	9%	20%	16%
Switzerland	8%	22%	4%	3%	1%	10%	31%	30%
Taiwan	51%	8%	2%	33%	10%	8%	6%	26%
United Kingdom	13%	23%	6%	6%	1%	29%	25%	11%
United States	12%	30%	9%	5%	2%	24%	14%	19%

differences in Table 2.2: the rate in Canada is nearly double that of the United States, even though its level of development is virtually the same. So cultural factors clearly play a strong role, even in countries with high national income.

While it is true that many Millennials live at home, from what we have seen, Millennials are generally no happier with their parents being actively involved in their work lives than their bosses are. In many cases, it appears that the parents are inserting themselves into their children's lives despite being told not to interfere. For example, one manager in India told us about having issues with employees' fathers and how she deals with them:

> *One employee of mine had to work late with her team on a project. She lives with her family (which is quite common in India) and told them she would be working late. The first night she worked until past 11 p.m. and then took a company car home. When she arrived home after midnight, her father was furious that she had come home so late and worried the whole family. She apologized and said that it was because her whole team was working late to meet a deadline. She explained that she would be working late for a few more nights and not to worry. The next night she got a call from the front desk at her office at 11 p.m. Her father had sent the family car for her, and she was expected to leave immediately. (Having a family driver is not unusual for the professional class in India.) She was embarrassed but left, apologizing to her team—and to me (her manager). The next day I received a call from her father, angry with me about his daughter having to work so late. I explained that if he didn't want her to lose her job, he needed to allow her to work the hours she needed to work to be successful and to not interfere. He could certainly send the car but not pull her away from her work. I told him that I understood his concern for her safety, but she's an adult and needed to be allowed to behave as such!*

While Millennials may share a great deal with their parents, they don't necessarily want them intimately involved in their work lives. And in many cases, the parental intrusion may be as embarrassing to Millennials as it is annoying to their bosses!

The Point

Millennials may want their parents to help them but don't want them to be actively involved in all parts of their work. It is a good idea for organizations to provide information that anyone (including parents) can use to understand the organization. But it is not necessary—or even desired by most Millennials—for an organization to include parents in the hiring process and other aspects of the employment relationship.

Millennials Are Needy . . . They Want Constant Mentoring and Support

While Millennials don't want their parents to take an active (interfering) role in their work lives, they do want support. Millennials perceive mentors as a support in their careers. They believe that a mentor will help them better negotiate the organization, plan their career, and open doors for them. Ninety-one percent of Millennials say they either have or want a mentor (the remaining 9 percent say they don't like their current mentor or don't want one).

Millennials' desire for a mentor is not new, and this desire is just as common among the older generations. Almost a decade ago, the book *Retiring the Generation Gap* reported that Millennials (and Baby Boomers and Gen Xers):[9]

- Wanted a mentor.
- Wanted a senior colleague, an expert in the field, or a coach they choose themselves as a mentor.
- Wanted the mentor to focus on their career, their leadership development, or their job.
- Overwhelmingly wanted the mentor relationship to take place face-to-face (a relationship only over the phone or other electronic medium was not desired).

This desire for a mentor likely comes from Millennials' belief that the purpose of the mentoring relationship is to focus on their needs as individuals, rather than on the organization's or team's needs. While supervisors can act as mentors, there is always the concern that supervisors will filter all advice, emphasizing what is best for themselves, the organization, or the team they manage. The same is not true of a mentor. Mentors may be thinking about how they can best help the individual to advance the ends of the organization, but their focus is still on the individual's development and what will be mutually beneficial.

In addition to wanting mentors, Millennials want their bosses to provide support when they have too much to do. Almost three-quarters[10] say immediate supervisors should go out of their way to help team members when demands become too difficult. What this means is that Millennials expect their supervisors to help get the work done when Millennials have too much to do. It is likely that expressing this attitude makes Millennials seem needy.

This wouldn't be an issue if there weren't a discrepancy between what the Millennials get from their supervisors and what they think they should be getting. While 73 percent of Millennials expect their supervisors to help, only 57 percent report that their supervisors do. So 16 percent perceive supervisors as not helping out as much as Millennials believe they should.

It is critical for organizations to pay attention to this discrepancy between what Millennials want and what they experience. Regardless of the actual levels of support, the gap between what Millennials believe supervisors should do and what they report supervisors actually do has a negative effect on their organizational commitment and engagement—and on the organization's performance over time.

The Point

Like all generations before them, Millennials want mentoring in the workplace. They want someone to whom they can turn for advice and help in navigating the workplace. One out of every six Millennials also wants their supervisors to help more with the work than they do currently. Millennials will be more engaged if they feel that they are getting enough mentoring in general, and enough support from their manager in particular.

Millennials Are Needy . . . They Want Frequent Feedback

Millennials are often described as needy because they want frequent feedback. They want to know how they are doing on a regular basis. This desire is following the tradition of Baby Boomers and Gen Xers, who challenged their bosses and organizations to provide more and better feedback for employees. It is consistent with Millennials' experience because many of them have grown up in a world where they received frequent feedback about how they were doing. In school and university, grades on papers, tests, and quizzes provided ongoing feedback. During nonschool time, feedback was frequent as well, from activities such as playing sports and interacting with friends (either face-to-face or virtually).

The world of social networking and texting has made it so feedback is typically available whenever an individual wants it. On Facebook, Instagram, and other social networks, people post pictures or notes about their personal lives and receive instantaneous "likes" and comments from their friends. Video games also provide constant feedback. Players win a race, rack up points, move up levels, etc. Anyone engaged in these kinds of activities receives constant feedback.

Joke

What do Millennials like to eat for breakfast?
Instant Feedback Loops

For some people, that feedback becomes as necessary as food. Then they get to the workplace. While there is assessment of performance at work, often feedback at work isn't as constant, as immediate, or as positive as some would like. And sometimes it is missing altogether. For example, one Millennial told us about a project he was on:

Our team created a report for a VP who asked for it. He thanked us, but then that was it. None of us on the team were told what he did with it or what the client thought. We didn't hear whether it was good or bad or how it could be done better in the future. It didn't come up at our end-of- year performance review. It was like we had done the work and then had dropped it into a black hole. We assume the work had helped the company, but we have no idea how. How can we improve if we don't get feedback? How can we feel motivated to do good work if we don't know how it is used or connected with the organization's goals? How can we feel appreciated if we aren't recognized for good work?

Lack of feedback is a common theme we heard while speaking with Millennials. The Millennials we studied were either at work or involved with work in one way or another 8 to 12 hours a day, at least five days a week, and often on weekends as well. With all of those hours at work, how frequently do you think they get feedback? A few times a day? Every day? Every week? No. Most say they get it quarterly (26 percent), a couple of times a year (34 percent), or only once a year (17 percent). While 54 percent of Millennials would like developmental feedback monthly or more frequently (daily or weekly), only 23 percent say they get feedback that frequently.

© Ron Leishman, ToonClipart.com

Rewards or recognition are even less frequent. Millennials would like rewards and recognition for their good work either monthly (25 percent) or quarterly (31 percent). They say they generally get rewards and recognition annually (51 percent) or twice a year (22 percent). What all these numbers boil down to is that Millennials aren't getting feedback, recognition, or rewards anywhere close to as frequently as they want, and that bothers them a great deal. They aren't asking for feedback as frequently as they get it socially or when playing video games, but they do want it more frequently than they are currently getting it.

If Millennials appear to be needy, perhaps it is because their managers aren't providing enough direction. Managers need to remember to set clear expectations for work and not assume anything. The management book *The One Minute Manager*[11] points out how quick and easy it is to provide both recognition and feedback to subordinates. Doing so doesn't have to take a lot of time. In fact, if it is done more frequently it is likely to take less time because the relationship is better established and there is less ramp-up time to the conversation. When feedback is provided immediately or soon after a relevant experience, the learning is more likely to stick—and you don't have to spend extra time reminding both sides of the reason for the conversation.

The bottom line is that most Millennials are working with people 40-plus hours a week (plus work outside of standard office hours), and yet most receive feedback or recognition no more frequently than every few months. That doesn't come close to meeting their needs. Millennials want relevant feedback about their performance frequently enough so they can act on it. If that makes them needy, then, yes, Millennials are needy—and with good reason.

The Point

Millennials want feedback about their work more frequently than they are currently receiving it. Managers should work on making sure that employees receive feedback at least every other week about the work they are doing. The door should be left open for employees to ask for feedback about their work if they are wondering how something went. The feedback doesn't need to be extensive; often an acknowledgement of the work is enough. But managers do need to provide some sort of frequent feedback.

Millennials Are Less Happy than Older Generations

One reason Millennials may seem needy is that they're not terribly happy. Less than a third[12] say that they look forward to each new day at work, and they scored lower than all older generations on a variety of positive measures, such as being enthusiastic, active, excited, and inspired. They also scored higher than all older generations on a variety of negative measures, such as feeling scared, upset, hostile, afraid, irritable, etc. In short, Millennials aren't particularly happy (see Figure 2.3).

FIGURE 2.3: Positive and Negative Affect Scale (PANAS)

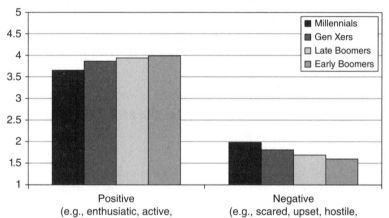

It is unexpected to find that people in their twenties and early thirties are less happy than their colleagues in their forties, fifties, and sixties, because the research on what is called the "U-bend of life" suggests that people in their twenties and early thirties typically would be happier than their older colleagues.[13,14] It is possible that this result is specific to our sample of professionals, managers, and executives. It is also possible that Millennials will have a different pattern over their life span. Researchers will continue to investigate the phenomenon.

Needy Does Not Mean Dependent

While Millennials want support, feedback, mentoring, and appreciation, that doesn't make them dependent. They actually are being quite strategic. They think about what they need to be successful, and that's what they ask for.

Millennials believe that they have no choice but to be independent actors in their careers. Baby Boomers grew up watching their parents (the World War II generation) in a work world characterized by long organizational tenure, secure pension plans, and organizational loyalty (employees staying with one organization for a long time were rewarded with steady, if slow, promotion). Millennials grew up in a different world altogether. They saw their parents (many of whom are Baby Boomers) deal with long hours, cutthroat competition, layoffs, wage stagnation, and insecure retirement plans. They witnessed the consequences of employees not having an independent attitude toward work. They saw dependence on an organization as an invitation to be taken advantage of, rather than something that is rewarded. As a consequence, they are independent: they want control over their work, don't trust or defer to authority much, and want their work to be flexible.

Millennials Are Independent . . . They Want Control over What They Are Doing

One way Millennials demonstrate their independence is through their desire to control their work lives and careers. Though they might want coaching and mentoring, Millennials don't want to be told what to do and don't like being expected to execute like automatons. Following the path established decades ago by the Baby Boomers and Gen Xers, Millennials don't see themselves as cogs in a giant machine; they see themselves as people who will shape their world to be what they want it to be.

For example, we were told about one Millennial nearing the end of a one-year rotation program during which she had three assignments in different departments to build her skills and capabilities so she could move up within the organization. As her program was ending, she was presented with a couple of different options for permanent roles. She didn't like either of them, so she turned them both down. She didn't accept the first because she didn't think the executive responsible for the group understood her development needs. She declined the second because she didn't think it aligned with her long-term career goals. She told the executive she was concerned that she didn't have a future with the company because the opportunities she was presented with were not ones she felt would further her career.

As in this example, Millennials want to actively take control of their careers and work assignments. Ninety-nine percent of Millennials (and 99 percent of older employees) say that having control over work assignments is important to them. Unfortunately, Millennials don't feel that they have control because they don't believe they are told what they need to know for their work or their career. They ask questions but aren't provided with the necessary information. In fact, a majority think their supervisors are not candid about why they are assigned specific work.

Millennials don't think this is a general communication breakdown. They believe most supervisors don't put a high priority on providing them with career-relevant information. While 61 percent of Millennials say they have enough information about how to accomplish their work related to the team's goals, almost the same percentage (58 percent) say *the reason* for their particular part of the work was not clearly explained to them. From their perspective, supervisors are better at communicating when the information advances immediate objectives or team goals, and are less effective at communicating information when the information is more general or helps Millennials' understand where their careers are going.

For example, a manager will be quite specific about the timeline for delivery of a project. But then five minutes later he might say that he will "have to see" when in the future the Millennial will be eligible for a developmental opportunity or promotion. The lack of specific communication regarding Millennials' future with the organization is unsettling to them. There is a "trust us" factor implied by the interaction, yet the organization is providing no reason for Millennials to trust that their needs will be met.

Addressing Millennials' desire for control does not have to be difficult. The key is that they want *more* control, not *full* control. They know it's unreasonable to expect complete autonomy in deciding what work they will do and how to do it. They want more information about the choices for their assignments, and the latitude to decide how to get the work done. Where appropriate, they also want the latitude to decide what work they will be doing. All employees want to be able to influence what work they are doing and how their work is performed.

The Point

Millennials feel like they have little or no control over their careers, and they want more control than they feel they currently have. Managers can help improve employees' feelings of control by providing more latitude for their employees to choose how and where work is done, by providing more information about why individuals are selected to do specific work, and by helping employees understand how their current work fits into their career plans more broadly.

Millennials Are Independent . . . They May Not Trust or Defer to Authority

Trust is a critical part of the workplace, but Millennials don't have unwavering trust in the people above them in their organizations.[15] This is not a new phenomenon and has been around for as long as young people have been challenging the norm of unquestioning

faith in institutions and organizations. Part of the reason Millennials are so independent is that they aren't particularly trusting in
general and of authority in particular.

For example, we heard a story from an executive about a time
he made a request of a Millennial. He couldn't find one of his
directors, so he asked someone two levels down in the organizational hierarchy to create a simple spreadsheet that day for a
meeting with a senior vice president the next day. He made sure
the Millennial didn't have any questions about what was needed
or when he needed it and went on with his day. The next morning he hadn't received the spreadsheet, so he checked in with
the Millennial and was told that he hadn't started working on it
yet. The Millennial's manager (the direct report of the executive
making the request) had been out the previous afternoon, and
the Millennial was waiting on his approval. The Millennial didn't
believe he should do the work without the approval of his supervisor, regardless of the fact that it was his supervisor's boss who
had asked for it. The executive said, "I was gobsmacked first that
he thought I was requesting versus assigning work, and second
that he believed that my direct report needed to OK work I had
assigned."

Examples like this highlight an interesting pattern that we
found: a majority[16] of Millennials (and almost three-quarters of
older employees[17]) don't think that employees in general or they
themselves in particular should do what their manager tells
them to do if they can't see the reason for it. This is likely rooted
partly in a lack of trust. Millennials don't have a great deal of
trust in people at work, and even less in the organization they
work for.

If Millennials don't trust the people in charge, it is logical
that they would be less likely to do what a manager or higher-level executive tells them to do without checking with
their immediate manager first. Why would they do something
if they can't see the reason for it, don't believe that employees have a duty to go along with the wishes of their manager
(or their manager's manager), and don't believe that obedience

TABLE 2.3 Millennials and Trust

38% of Millennials say that they trust their boss a lot,
while 8% say they do not trust their boss *at all*.
33% say that they trust the people they work with a lot,
while 4% say they don't trust them *at all*.
28% say that they trust their CEO a lot,
while 10% say they don't trust the CEO *at all*.
24% say that they trust their organization a lot,
while 7% say they don't trust their organization *at all*.

to supervisors at work is desirable? Given the lack of trust and cultural shifts in the past 40 years, it makes sense that Millennials would not follow every directive given by their superiors within the organization.

The larger question is why this lack of trust exists. Leaders and managers sometimes forget that employees willingly follow the people they respect, think are honest, and feel treat them fairly. As Baby Boomers pointed out years ago and Gen Xers reiterated, trust in leadership does not come simply from leaders having a higher-level role than those they supervise. The leaders have to continuously earn their direct reports' trust. And that comes from a combination of being honest, leading by example, demonstrating relevant knowledge, and giving people the room to succeed or fail on their own, with appropriate accountability, consequences, and rewards for performance. Often, employees don't believe that their leaders and managers at every level embody these characteristics and behaviors.

Not trusting authority doesn't mean that Millennials reject structure in an organization. In fact, a majority of Millennials think structure in an organization is important and say that they want there to be a clear chain of command and lines of authority (for more on this, see Chapter 1).

While Millennials want an organizational structure, they don't want a boss who orders people around just because he or she has the authority to do so. Happily, a majority (64 percent) of Millennials say they don't have that kind of boss. Unfortunately, 16 percent of Millennials say that their boss does behave this way—and 20 percent aren't willing to say one way or the other. What this means is that 16 percent of Millennials are working for people they perceive as abusing their authority—and an additional 20 percent may be. So more than a third of Millennials may be seeing their bosses behave poorly. And even if the organization is addressing the supervisor's bad behavior behind the scenes, Millennials care about how they are being treated more than they do about organizational initiatives that may address the problem eventually. When the bad behavior continues, it reflects poorly on the entire organization and its leaders.

The Point

Millennials are not wholly trusting of authority. Like older employees, they dislike working for people who exert their authority arbitrarily. Managers shouldn't order employees around just because they can, regardless of the employees' age. Managers should provide enough direction and information regarding required work to satisfy the employee. At the same time, if some Millennials don't do their jobs, their managers should hold them accountable. No one, including Millennials, wants to pull the weight of colleagues who leave it to others to do their jobs for them.

Millennials Are Independent . . . They Want to Have Flexibility at Work

Millennials are quite independent in their work style. For example, 99 percent of Millennials say that it is important to have autonomy in getting their work done. Part of autonomy for Millennials is having the flexibility to work where and when they want to, while still being productive.

Millennials and Overall Trust

Millennials' lack of trust extends beyond the workplace. When asked whether they believe that most people can be trusted,

- 32 percent of Millennials say people can be trusted.
- 24 percent say you can't be too careful dealing with people.
- 44 percent say it depends.

In other words, only about one-third of the Millennials included in our research believe that people in general can be trusted, which is less than the 44 percent of older employees who say that people can be trusted.[18]

That number is supported by answers to other questions we asked about whether they trust the police in their own community (15 percent don't), whether they trust the media (35 percent don't), and whether they trust the banking industry (29 percent don't).

When it comes to people in their communities, Millennials aren't particularly trusting either. Less than 15 percent of Millennials say that they trust the people in their neighborhood or their community a lot. Further, only about a third[19] say that they trust the people in their place of worship, and a paltry 13 percent say they trust those with whom they share their religious beliefs. (Older people are slightly more trusting on average.[20])

Why are Millennials not particularly trusting of the people around them? Some have suggested it is because Millennials feel they themselves are not trusted because of how they are treated in the workplace. Our data show that Millennials who report feeling someone thinks they are dishonest are less trusting—of their bosses, their CEOs, their organizations, and the people they work with. Therefore, managers need to demonstrate to Millennial employees that they are trusted. To send that message, managers should provide them with flexibility, not micromanage them, and give them additional responsibilities.

For example, a focus group of Millennials in the United States was asked what bothered them about their work. Partway through the focus group, one particularly high-achieving Millennial got very upset. Why? Her boss wasn't allowing her to go to her 7 pm yoga class. This was particularly upsetting to her because going to the yoga class was an important part of her life—it was how she managed her stress. When her boss said she couldn't go, she said she would come back and work until midnight to "make up the time" she missed to go to her class. The work she was doing was independent of anyone else, so as long as she got it done, why did she have to miss something that was important to her? The perspective of the boss was that she was part of the team and needed to stay in the office without a break to show support for the team.

This wasn't a generational conflict—the boss was a Millennial just four years older than she. This was a conflict over differences in perception, the need for autonomy, and beliefs about flexibility at work. The employee didn't see why the hour of additional face time at 7 p.m. was necessary for the work; her boss thought it was. In the end, she didn't go to yoga because she was concerned about the negative effect it would have on her boss's perception of her as well as on her career prospects.

Millennials think that autonomy and flexibility mean working where and when they want so they can meet their personal needs—as long as they are being productive. Nowadays, working remotely using a computer or mobile device is easy. Because it is so easy and anyone can do it in principle, flexibility is perceived as just part of the job that everyone should have, rather than a perk to be earned. Older workers remember a time when leaving work early or working at home was a perk rather than an expectation. They often are annoyed by many smartphone-carrying workers—especially Millennials who are new to an organization—who believe that their work schedules should always be flexible, rather than seeing flexibility as a right that is earned.

Millennials disagree. They are part of a decades-long tradition of pushing organizations to increase workplace flexibility. They are independent workers who enjoy autonomy and don't believe that spending time in the office indicates they are being productive. Given that 91 percent are contacted about work outside of work hours, clearly their bosses and coworkers don't think that being in the office is required to get work done either. The frequency of contact about work outside of work hours means that they are already working flexibly to accommodate the organization's needs (for more on this, see Chapter 1). So why shouldn't they be able to work flexibly to meet their own needs?

When asked whether flexibility was important to them, Millennials overwhelmingly answered *yes*:

- 95 percent said that occasionally doing work from home (or wherever they want to be) is important to them.
- 96 percent said that occasionally shifting their work hours later or earlier to accommodate their personal life was important to them.

Flexibility does have some downsides. There is the issue of face time, which is important for learning, bonding with teams, and being seen to be productive. When people work flexibly, they have to show they are so productive and committed to the organization that they are available whenever necessary, even if they aren't in the office. This can pose a challenge to those who want to have some uninterrupted personal time. But it appears that Millennials are willing to take on this challenge in exchange for the autonomy they enjoy and the flexibility to meet their personal needs.

The Point

Millennials want workplace flexibility. They want to have the latitude to be someplace other than at work, as long as it doesn't affect their productivity. Managers should provide such flexibility as much as possible. Part of providing flexibility is having planning conversations with employees about deliverables so everyone is on the same page and working toward the same goals and timelines.

Conclusion: Millennials Are Both Needy and Independent Because They're Goal-Oriented

As you can see, the evidence shows that Millennials may be needy, but they are also fiercely independent. Millennials are both needy and independent simultaneously because they are focused on improving their work experiences and their career trajectories. They are needy because they realize they need assistance from those around them to improve. They are independent because they don't trust those same people to make their best interests a priority.

One way Millennials are simultaneously needy and independent is in their desire to learn. Because they understand the work world they have entered and think that they are disposable to any organization, they strongly believe that they have to be continuous learners and can't allow their skills to stagnate. They don't expect to be able to stay in one job for 30 years and do the same thing over and over again (even if they wanted to). Instead, they believe that they have to keep growing, learning, and contributing more and different things to the organization. In fact, lack of learning opportunities is one of the reasons they will leave (see Chapter 5 for more information).

Given that Millennials are simultaneously needy and independent, the following sections describe some actions you can take to work more effectively with them, whether you are a team member, a manager, or a leader.

How Different Are Millennials, Really?

On average, parents of Millennials are likely to be more involved in their adult children's work lives than the parents of older staff were. And when it comes to sharing information on compensation, even Millennials who are married and have children are more likely to share with their parents than are members of older generations. While parents are more involved in Millennials' work lives, there is general agreement among Millennials, Gen Xers, and Baby Boomers that having parents very involved in their adult children's work lives isn't desirable.

Millennials are similar to older generations in their desire to have mentors, to get frequent feedback, to feel appreciated, to have control over their work, and to receive help when they need it. Millennials are slightly less trusting of most people they interact with at work and in their personal lives than are older generations.

Recommendations for Working with Millennials as Team Members

Some older team members worry that Millennials want them to act like parents. Not to worry—they don't. Millennials have their own parents to worry about. What they would appreciate, however, is a helpful older mentor who can provide feedback on how they are doing and how to be more organizationally savvy. Millennials realize that their older peers have knowledge that they didn't learn in school, and they appreciate it when this knowledge is shared. They won't necessarily act as you'd like them to, but they do appreciate the information.

What Millennials don't appreciate is being told that a task needs to be done a particular way because it has always been done that way. There is a big difference to Millennials between saying something like, "You might want to try it this way because I've found it saves me a lot of time and effort in the long run, but of course it is your choice," versus "You should do it this way because this is the way it's been done for a long time and it works well enough." Remember, Millennials don't like boring work and don't want their time wasted, so how long a process has been used is not a good rationale for continuing it; they need to understand the logical reasons for it.

Millennials appreciate the opportunity to learn new things, which means that they are likely to want to learn about what you're doing and help you with it. This is also why they appreciate positive mentoring. They understand that they don't know everything, even though they may appear very sure of themselves; they realize there are many things they have to learn at work. In fact, they want to learn—it makes work more interesting and keeps it from getting too boring and routine.

One key to working with Millennials lies in striking the right balance between telling them what to do and being supportive of their independent action. Help them understand what they don't know and provide them opportunities to learn from you. Hopefully, at the same time, you'll also find some areas where you can learn from them. They do have considerable knowledge; thinking in terms of what you can learn from each other can improve your relationship. They are likely to be open to and interested in your input. So approach them as peers and appeal to their desire to learn new things, while also appealing to their desire to avoid doing things that waste their time and create rework. Acting superior is a surefire route to turning them off and creating conflict instead of allies.

Recommendations for Managing Millennials (and Everyone Else)

1. Don't worry about managing their parents.
Most Millennials don't want their parents to be intimately involved in their work life any more than Gen Xers or Baby Boomers do. Does this mean you will never encounter an intrusive parent of a Millennial? Unfortunately, you might. But if you do, you should treat it like any unusual, out-of-bounds behavior. All employees can have family members—whether parents, a spouse, or a sibling—who find ways to interject themselves into work processes where they aren't invited. Employees usually don't want them involved but may have a little difficulty navigating the situation entirely on their own. And even if they have it under control, some compassionate words and support from you can go a long way toward smoothing things over and minimizing any potential embarrassment the employee might

feel. If you happen to be managing the very rare Millennial who thinks it's perfectly fine for his or her parents to get involved in the workplace, the best thing you can do is clearly and unequivocally, but gently, explain the bounds of appropriate behavior.

2. Let them know how they are doing—frequently. Provide them with mentors and frequent feedback.

The simple truth is that most employees receive too little feedback in organizations today, regardless of their generation. Virtually every role in every organization would benefit from greater and more frequent feedback and guidance. You need to work toward that goal, not because it's a good employment practice for your Millennial employees but because everyone, young and old alike, would benefit from more frequent and detailed feedback.

Therefore, as a manager, look for opportunities to provide feedback at appropriate times, not just at regularly scheduled intervals once a year or at the end of a project. Employees want both to know how they are doing and to feel appreciated on a consistent basis, not just when the work is done. If their work falls short of what you consider to be acceptable, they will respond much better if they are told in the moment when they have a chance to fix things rather than afterward, when the immediate opportunity to demonstrate improvement has passed. And if they are doing uninteresting work, you should take special care to let them know how they are doing and that their contribution is valued (see Chapter 1).

3. Provide support when things get tough.

Most employees want and need independence to do their work and don't welcome being micromanaged. It is important to give all staff—including Millennials—the opportunity to succeed on their own, or else they will never develop the self-confidence needed to operate at higher levels within the organization. Yet independence and being totally cut off from all support are two very different things.

As a manager, make sure that employees have the time and space to work on and accomplish their tasks on their own. However, if you see that their work is subpar, provide them with support quickly so that they can correct their work and learn from their mistakes. Employees will not only benefit from learning from their mistakes; their self-esteem and business performance will be more shielded from risk.

4. Let them control as much as possible.

Control at work can be a tricky thing. People want to have a voice in determining what work they will do and choosing opportunities for the future. They also want to determine how and where they do their work. Of course, you can't let people change every aspect of their work on a whim because there are too many proven processes that have to be followed in order for work to be done efficiently and effectively. However, in most roles, there is often room for individuals to control a great deal of how they do their work.

As a manager, giving your employees the freedom and control to determine parts of their job duties and work processes is a key to heightened engagement, commitment, and productivity. Communicate clearly and often with them about goals, timelines, and expectations for performance. Then give them the time, space, and autonomy to make decisions about work processes where there is some discretion in how things are done. Doing so will make them much happier and more committed to working for you in both the short and longer term.

5. Trust and be trustworthy.

Millennials might not be particularly trusting, but our data show that they will feel more trusting if they feel trusted. Give them some control over their work, listen to their thoughts, and provide the right kinds of support. Don't disregard their ideas, and don't micromanage them. Support them with the tools, resources, and colleagues needed to get the job done in an efficient and effective manner. Show that you trust them to get the job done.

Employees today have very sensitive lie detectors. They can sense when people are being inauthentic or dishonest. Though managers can't always tell the complete truth, they need to be aware that people are sensitive to a leader or manager saying one thing at one point in time and then doing something different later. If there is a chance a communication might be perceived this way, it may be better to say nothing at all or explain that you can't say anything rather than open yourself to the potential criticism that you weren't entirely honest.

Five Points to Remember

1. Millennials want to control their lives and work as much as possible.
2. Millennials want to know what they need to do to be successful.
3. Millennials don't want to be told precisely how to do everything.
4. Millennials are more likely to trust when they feel trusted.
5. Millennials don't want their parents too involved.

Who Millennials Are and What They Want

Millennials:
- Don't want their parents involved, even if they live with them
- Want mentors and support
- Want frequent feedback
- Want assistance where it is needed and expect people to pitch in to help
- Want to be appreciated
- Want control over what they are doing
- May not trust or defer much to authority
- Are very goal-oriented

CHAPTER 3

DO GOOD *AND* DO WELL

Janice is a Millennial who was working for a midsize nonprofit in the arts. When she was 23 she started working for the organization because she believed in its mission to make arts programs available to the broader community. Her original job was a 30-hour-a-week, hourly position that involved helping with community outreach and fund-raising. Over the next two years, her role expanded because she was committed, hardworking, and quite good at it. By the time she was 25, she was in charge of fund-raising and was managing many of the community outreach efforts. She often took on initiatives in her free time just because they needed to be done. For example, she completely redesigned the organization's website because she had noticed it wasn't easy for people to buy tickets to performances. Over the two years she worked for the organization, she had received a $1-an-hour raise, but she couldn't get the organization to give her full-time hours because it didn't want to pay for her benefits. Because she had no health insurance through the organization, she had stayed on her parents' policy. As her twenty-sixth birthday approached,[1] she began thinking about whether she could stay with the organization. She wanted to continue her work there because she saw it and the organization as making a real contribution to the community. She asked again to be brought on full time so that she could get health benefits and begin to save for retirement, but the organization's leaders said they didn't want to do that. They said she should be happy with the small raise and the large impact she was having on the community. But she knew it wouldn't be financially responsible to stay at her current compensation level, especially with the lack of benefits. She

had bills to pay, health care to think about, and retirement to save
for. Reluctantly, she looked for another job. She found one quickly
with another arts organization that had a community outreach pro-
gram she could participate in. With the new job, she received a more
accurate title, greater scope and authority, 40 percent more pay, full
medical benefits, and a retirement plan.

MILLENNIALS WANT TO DO GOOD IN THE WORLD, RIGHT?

Do Millennials want to save the world? Yes. Is saving the world a
higher priority than comfort and compensation? Not so much. Is it
important to them? Yes. Will they give up pay for it? Maybe some,
maybe for a while, but not forever. But is doing good a priority for
them? Absolutely.

How do they want to do good? By making a contribution to the
community, working for a socially responsible organization, and
thinking beyond their immediate community.

Millennials Want to Do Good . . . by Making a Contribution to the Community

Millennials believe that their work should make a contribution to
the world, not just make them money. Ninety-two percent say that
making the world a better place is at least somewhat important
to them. Eighty-eight percent of Millennials think that getting
involved in community and charity efforts is at least somewhat
important.

These percentages show us that Millennials want to help; the
question is why. A study published by the organization Achieve in
2013 found that Millennials gave a number of reasons they chose
to volunteer. When asked, 79 percent of Millennials said it was
because they were passionate about the issue, 56 percent said it
was because they wanted to meet new people who were interested in the same issues, and 61 percent said it was to broaden
their professional skills.[2,3] So even when doing good, Millennials

are thinking about how it fits in with their career strategy and how they as individuals can benefit from the volunteering.

Interestingly, Achieve's 2014 research, which was done with a U.S. sample, found that 63 percent of Millennials did not consider time set aside for volunteering during work hours when looking for a job. Instead, they focused on the specifics of the organization's work (e.g., the products and services) and the specifics of the job (e.g., pay and benefits).[4] More than half of Millennials who did discuss volunteering (either because their interviewer brought it up or because they did) said knowing about the volunteering options made them more likely to take the job. (Note: While this is true in the United States, laws about volunteering vary substantially across countries. Millennials' views are shaped by their country's rules on taking work time to volunteer in the community.)

Achieve's study found that female Millennials were more focused on and affected by this opportunity than were their male peers.[5] Achieve reported that

> *Overall, female Millennials were more likely than male Millennials to both donate money to and volunteer for causes they care about. In 2013, 91 percent of the female Millennial employees we surveyed donated to charities, compared to 84 percent of the male Millennial employees. Female Millennial employees were also more likely to participate in company-sponsored employee giving campaigns. Of the female Millennial employees surveyed, 54 percent had given through a company-sponsored giving campaign, compared to 45 percent of male Millennial employees.*[6]

Millennials don't want to help only as individuals; they think organizations should want to help their communities as well, and 97 percent believe it is important to work for an employer that shares their values. The good news is that the majority of Millennials believe that their organizations are socially responsible. Specifically, three-quarters (75 percent) say that their organization is a good citizen in the community. In a 2014 study,

Achieve reported that 92 percent felt they were working for "a company that was having a positive effect on the world."[7]

Millennials also believe that helping the community should be important to managers. Specifically, 77 percent believe that making the world a better place should be important to managers, 78 percent believe that being of service to society should be important to managers, and 73 percent believe that contributing to humanity should be important to managers. Happily, our data indicate that non-Millennial managers and executives have perspectives quite similar to those of Millennials (see Figure 3.1).

The Point

Millennials truly care about making a contribution to the community, and a majority believe that their organization is doing that. Many Millennials would appreciate the opportunity to do volunteer work in their community as part of their job. Managers who share their beliefs about volunteering in the community can connect with Millennials on that subject, and can help them understand how their work contributes. Organizations should look for ways to improve how they contribute to the community.

FIGURE 3.1: Percentage Who Believe Certain Values Are Important (by Age Group)

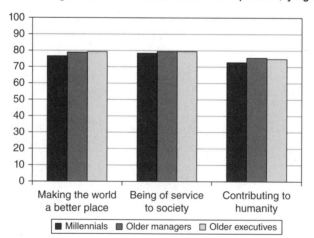

Millennials Want to Do Good . . . by Working for a Socially Responsible Organization

Millennials care about their impact on the world, and they want to work for companies that maximize the positive impact and minimize the negative impact of their operations. While half of Millennials say that they stay with their organization for the career opportunities, a third[8] say that they stay because they believe in the mission of the organization. In our experience, those who say they are thinking about compensation and career opportunities consider the mission as well.

Our story about Janice at the beginning of this chapter is a good example. She cares about doing good, which is why she works for an organization in whose mission she believes. When she must leave the organization that can't meet her financial needs, she goes to another socially oriented organization that has a mission aligned with her values *and* can meet her financial needs.

The good news is that Millennials are receptive to the good-citizen efforts many organizations are implementing. Three-quarters say their organization is a good citizen in the community, and more than half[9] say their organization demonstrates a concern for the environment.

© Ron Leishman, ToonClipart.com

At the same time, while efforts to help the community and be more socially responsible are appreciated by Millennials, they are split on the question of whether the company is really focused on helping the community or is more interested in the good PR the organization can get from it. Only about half[10] of Millennials disagreed with the statement "My organization is more concerned about its image than really helping in the community." So about half[11] of Millennials think their organization may be involved in socially responsible practices simply to burnish its image.

This is problematic. Millennials want their organizations to act for the greater good (rather than for the PR benefit) in part because they believe that organizations that behave this way are more trustworthy and ethical. Achieve found that Millennials believe such an organizational culture will translate into a better day-to-day workplace environment.[12]

Finding the right amount and form of socially responsible action can take some effort on the part of the organization. The good news is that if you put in the time and energy to come up with meaningful socially responsible practices, Millennials likely will believe you are being genuine. That in turn will help them believe that the organization is trustworthy and ethical.

The Point

Millennials want their organizations to be good corporate citizens, and they want creating a better world to be part of the business plan. They value working for a socially responsible organization, one that does the work to do good more than to look good. Organizations that do this will benefit from increased commitment and retention among Millennials.

Millennials Want to Do Good . . . by Thinking Beyond Their Immediate Community

The interviews we conducted around the world revealed that Millennials often think a great deal about the world beyond their immediate community. They feel they need to learn about the broader world so that they can make a greater contribution. They believe they are doing good when they use their time at work to gain a greater understanding of people in other countries and cultures.

Many believe that this global focus is very different from their parents' generation. For example, we were told that in Europe, the post–World War II generation was viewed as much more conformist, taking what was given to them and questioning it less than workers do today. They also lived with a more locally focused perspective, seeing themselves as citizens primarily of their home country. According to this narrative, today's young European workers look much more at the entire European Union and global issues as relevant to their lives, taking a broader view instead of saying they are just French, German, Spanish, or U.K. citizens.

In Japan, we were told that younger people are more aware of their place in the world than are those only 15 years older. Millennials there said that they want to experience and learn from the world outside of Japan. They see themselves as part of a global group and aspire to be able to work anywhere.

Similarly, there is a sense in the United States that the world is much more flat today (to borrow a phrase from Thomas Friedman).[13] Millennials feel they need to take a more global view of the world they live and work in.

These views were not limited to the developed world. In India, China, Brazil, and South Africa, all of the Millennials we encountered were acutely aware of economic and political developments both at home and abroad. Today, information and cultural influences spread rapidly around the world via the Internet and social media. Clearly, this has played a role in shaping how Millennials see themselves as part of a global community. During the interviews and focus groups, there was a sense that Millennials were both quite attached to their home countries (in some cases, their home cities) and simultaneously quite interested in experiencing the world beyond their homes as much as possible.

For Millennials, having a global view includes both the willingness and the desire to work abroad. We found that 40 percent of Millennials said they wanted to have an assignment working in another country, though only 6 percent said they have already had the opportunity. That's good news for companies that struggle to find people willing to work in far-flung locations. But the overseas assignments are interesting primarily to Millennials who haven't put down roots yet. Once they have a spouse and a family, they are less inclined to take overseas assignments.

For example, we interviewed a number of Millennials in South Africa who were keen on having an international work experience. One Millennial we interviewed had just spent a couple of years working abroad. He was happy to be back home with his wife and was planning to start a family now that they were back near their relatives.

Other (younger) Millennials were itching to go overseas. They said they had traveled extensively but hadn't yet had the experience of really living and working in another country. Though they planned to return home to start families, they wanted to spend the next few years working overseas and learning about the world.

There are substantial differences globally in who wants international assignments. For example, the Millennials in Brazil were most likely to say they wanted an international assignment (65 percent), while the Millennials in the United Kingdom, Canada, and Japan were the least likely (28–29 percent; see Figure 3.2).

A note of caution about international assignments comes from some of the interviews we conducted. Company leaders were quick to point out that when Millennials think of global assignments, they often focus on cosmopolitan cities. The Millennials we spoke with said the same thing. Most wanted to move to places where they could learn and have an adventure, such as Paris, London, Rome, Hong Kong, and New York. But the reality of business today is that the greatest needs are in emerging markets, countries where the living is not so glamorous. Many Millennials are less excited about moving to countries that are still developing economically.

On the positive side, there are a handful of cosmopolitan emerging-market cities such as São Paulo, Shanghai, and Mumbai where Millennials are more likely to find a large group of peers with whom to socialize. But even these cities may not be the main

FIGURE 3.2: Percentage of Millennials Who Desire to Have an Assignment Working in Another Country

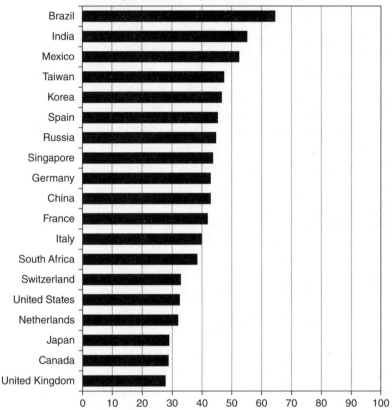

target for business expansion. The places with less cachet are often precisely where organizations need the most help. So there are limits to many organizations' ability to find a perfect match between the business need and Millennials' desire for global assignments.

The Point

Millennials want to experience and learn from parts of the world beyond their home countries. Provide Millennials with the opportunity to experience the world outside of their current homes, if they are interested. Where relevant, help Millennials understand how working in emerging markets can benefit them, the organization, and the community where they would be living.

DOING GOOD ISN'T A HIGHER PRIORITY THAN DOING WELL

Yes, Millennials think doing good is important. However, it isn't their only—or even highest—priority (see Figure 3.3). Ninety-two percent of Millennials believe their company has a positive effect on the world. On the other hand, only 34 percent say that they stay because of their company's mission. What that tells us is that doing good is important, but *by itself* it isn't a distinguishing enough factor for Millennials. (Note: Millennials and other generations are remarkably similar when it comes to the importance of doing good and staying because of the mission.)

What is very important? Compensation. Forty-three percent say it is extremely important, and 38 percent say it is very important. Overall, a massive 99 percent of Millennials we studied believe that their compensation is at least somewhat important. When do 99 percent of a generation agree on anything?

This is definitely a "both/and" situation—Millennials want work that both enables them to contribute to society in positive ways and rewards them appropriately. One is not a substitute for the other. You can't skimp on compensation just because your

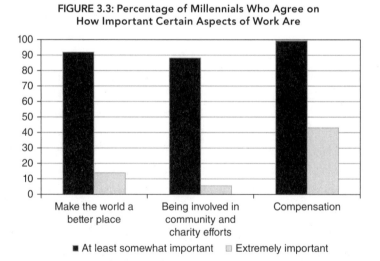

FIGURE 3.3: Percentage of Millennials Who Agree on How Important Certain Aspects of Work Are

organization makes some amazing contributions to the world either through your core business model or through your philanthropy. After all, most Millennials believe that their organizations are contributing and, as the example of Janice shows, they can move to other organizations that both make a contribution to the community and pay better. Therefore, emphasizing the organization's contributions to the community while being cheap on compensation isn't an effective strategy for attracting and retaining Millennials.

Experience with Economic Hardship May Have Long-Term Effects on Millennials

Even though many parts of the world, including the United States, have recovered substantially from the depths of the Great Recession that began in 2007, the effects of living through that economic event still linger in both concrete and emotional terms. Many jobs that disappeared never came back, and many industries that had strong growth in the mid-2000s have scaled back, especially finance and construction. The rate of long-term unemployment remains stubbornly high in many countries, especially among Millennials. Many Millennials entered the workforce during this bad economy, and many have had a difficult time finding a decent job.

Adding to the difficult job market and global slowdown are longer-term trends in economic insecurity and inequality that the Great Recession helped bring to the forefront of Millennials' minds (for more on this, see Chapter 7). Those trends, combined with the economic scars from the recession, have made many more nervous about their financial well-being than they were before the recession. Millennials especially have reason to be concerned about their compensation. The evidence shows that when a group enters the workforce during a recession, its members will make less over the course of their lives than they would have if they had begun working during a stronger economic period. As a consequence, the Millennial generation today may be unusually fixated on compensation and doing well enough financially to have a decent lifestyle—perhaps more fixated than we've seen since those who experienced the ravages of the Great Depression.

Millennials Want to Do Well . . . Because They Are Motivated Both by Work and by Social Comparison

In Chapter 1, we said that Millennials are more motivated by the work itself than they are by extrinsic rewards such as cash or reputation. While 81 percent of Millennials say that compensation is very or extremely important to them, only 29 percent say they are *motivated to work* specifically because it allows them to make a lot of money.

Millennials are intrinsically motivated: they do the work because it is interesting to them. They are interested in money, but it's not the primary reason they do the work. They do the work because they find it interesting and rewarding. At the same time, they are also very aware of compensation, both because it determines their standard of living and because it is an indicator of their progress. And understanding their progress and their place in the world of work is important to them.

When Millennials leave university, they leave a place where their grades showed them how well they had done. When they get to the workplace, they look for similar feedback. Though annual reviews certainly provide feedback about performance, they are much less tangible than compensation is. Compensation is the most direct indicator of how the organization perceives the value of an individual. While every person provides value to the organization (otherwise people wouldn't continue to have jobs), some people's skills are simply more critical for an organization to retain than are other people's skills. The people who are perceived as being more critical and whose skills are in greater demand outside the organization are typically paid more.

Millennials understand this and look to their compensation to see how they rank in the organization. They know that their peers who are paid more are viewed as more highly ranked. So Millennials frequently seek to find out how their compensation compares with that of others.

For comparisons outside the organization, they use websites that provide information about others' compensation (and provide information anonymously to others about their own compensation). The information is available by job, organization, and industry. Sixty percent of Millennials in our research said they had used these sites (as have 53 percent of older staff). Millennials are clearly well aware of these sites, perhaps more so than their bosses (more on this in Chapters 4 and 5).

In addition to looking for and sharing information anonymously and virtually, Millennials also discuss their compensation with other people directly. Only 6 percent say that they don't discuss their compensation with anyone—which means that 94 percent of Millennials overall are discussing their compensation with someone. Millennials are most likely to discuss their compensation with their parents (71 percent), their friends (47 percent), or their spouses (96 percent of those who have a spouse; see Figure 3.4). While more than half look at websites to see what others are making, less than half (38 percent) said that they discussed their compensation directly with coworkers. This pattern holds globally: fewer than half of Millennials share their compensation information with coworkers, except in the Netherlands, Spain, Brazil, Italy, and France (see Figure 3.5). Millennials are much more likely than their older peers to discuss their compensation directly with coworkers (see Appendix 3.1).

In addition to comparing their compensation, Millennials compare how they are doing in general—in life and work—to how others are doing. Much has been made of the use of Facebook and other social media for social comparison. The implication is that Millennials are less happy than previous generations because they compare their lives to those of their friends as portrayed on social media.[14] We find that the primary points of comparison appear to be friends from university (73 percent) and people from work (69 percent). Fifty-four percent use people in their professional

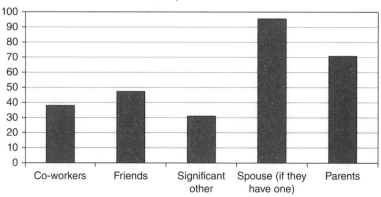

FIGURE 3.4: Percentage of Millennials Who Discuss
Their Compensation With:

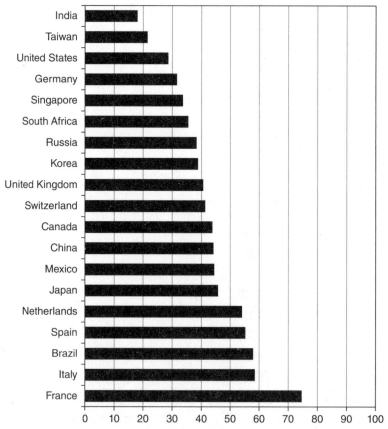

FIGURE 3.5: Percentage of Millennials Who Discuss
Their Compensation with Their Coworkers

network outside of their current organization as comparisons, and 51 percent say they compare themselves to social friends.

Another aspect of social comparison focuses on parents. People generally want to do at least as well as their parents did. And while there is considerable variability among countries (see Figure 3.6), a majority of Millennials (62 percent) believe that their financial standard of living will be higher than that of their parents. Unfortunately, only about 39 percent of Millennials believe that their quality of life will be higher than that of their parents (see Figure 3.7). It is likely that Millennials expect greater job demands and worse work-life balance throughout their careers (compared to their parents), and therefore anticipate that their quality of life will be lower even though they believe that they will be financially better off.

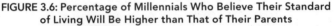

FIGURE 3.6: Percentage of Millennials Who Believe Their Standard of Living Will Be Higher than That of Their Parents

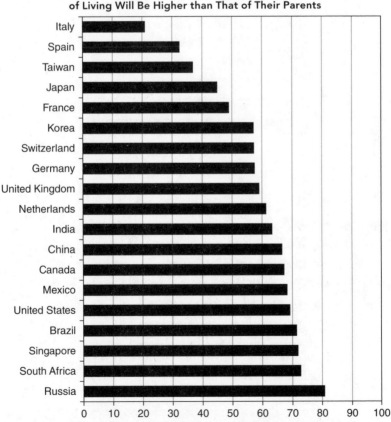

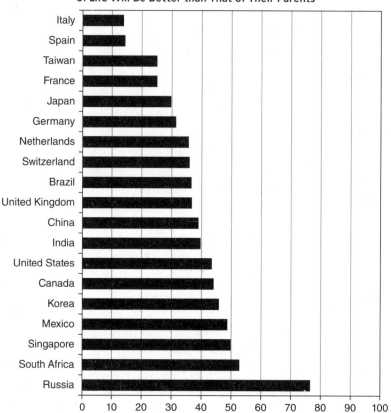

FIGURE 3.7: Percentage of Millennials Who Think Their Quality of Life Will Be Better than That of Their Parents

The Point

Millennials care about their compensation both for practical reasons and because they want to know how they measure up. They compare their pay with what people report on the Internet and what they hear from family, coworkers, and friends. While a majority think they will do better financially than their parents did, they don't think their quality of life will be as high; they expect to have to work harder and longer to be successful in their careers. Organizations need to pay Millennials appropriately and to realize that they are comparing their compensation with that of people at other organizations. Organizations shouldn't try to hide or skew where the compensation sits in the distribution, because Millennials are likely to find out.

Millennials Want to Do Well . . . Because They Are Concerned About Debt and Paying the Bills

The primary reason Millennials are so focused on compensation is they have bills to pay. Growing up and establishing a household separate from their parents is expensive.

Debt is a significant concern for many Millennials.[15] In fact, 46 percent of Millennials we surveyed say that financial debt directly affects their career decisions. Rather than leave their current work to get the development they need or take a less stable job in an area they are passionate about, many Millennials will stay in a job that isn't their preference because it pays their debts. We spoke with a number of Millennials who said they weren't in their dream jobs but they were paid so well that they didn't feel they could leave. They said that staying with the organization would allow them to pay off their loans more quickly, save enough to buy a place to live, and still be able to go out and have fun.

Source: CagleCartoons.com

Student Debt in the United States

In the United States, one common type of debt Millennials have is student loans. In 2013, 69 percent of Millennials graduating from university had student loans.[16] For many Millennials in the United States, payments on student loans are their single largest monthly expense, so a primary concern for them is whether their compensation is high enough to live on after they have made their loan payments every month.

While much has been said about high student debt in the United States, debt in general affects young employees around the world (see Figure 3.8).[17] The figure shows that the importance of debt in Millennials' job and career choices varies widely across countries. While only a small percentage of Millennials in our sample in Switzerland and Germany say debt affects their career choices, a majority of Millennials in Singapore, the United States, the United Kingdom, Russia, Spain, Italy, and France said it affected their career choices; in Canada, India, South Africa, Brazil, Taiwan, and China, almost half said the same.

For many households, housing debt is the biggest liability. Millennials who are just starting their careers and establishing families may not yet have housing debt. However, they cannot ignore the price of housing when making career decisions.

Housing prices have risen significantly over the last 15 or so years—about the same time the oldest Millennials started entering the workforce. Housing prices didn't rise just in the United States; they also rose in Europe,[18] making affordability a big issue for Millennials in many countries around the world (as it has always been in Singapore and Hong Kong).

In some countries, house prices are even less affordable than they are in the United States because the cost of buying is so much higher than the cost of renting. In other countries, including the United States, affordability has improved since the housing bubble burst with the Great Recession that began in 2007. Though housing

FIGURE 3.8: Percentage of Millennials Who Say Their Need to Repay Student Loans or Other Debt Affects Their Career Decisions

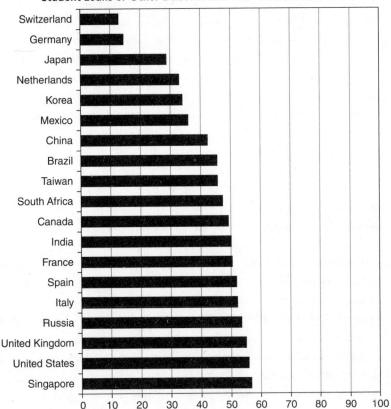

is more affordable, many young people have difficulty entering the market because of the down payment and credit rating require-ments for purchasing a home.[19] Others have difficulty finding a stable job or have income that isn't growing enough for them to enter the housing market.[20] In countries with this pattern, Millen-nials may currently have no way to purchase a home and therefore remain as renters or choose to live with their parents. (See Chapter 2 for more details on Millennials living with their parents.)

Whether Millennials are taking on more debt to afford their first house or choosing to rent or live with their parents, the prospect of high mortgage debt and concerns about income growth affect their life decisions, including choices they make about their careers (see

Figure 3.8). Older Millennials, particularly those thinking about starting a family, told us they were concerned about making sure they had saved enough to buy a place for their family to live.

The implications of debt concerns will be significant for this new generation of workers. Consider, for example, our discussion of entitlement from Chapter 1. More than 90 percent of Millennials want greater flexibility in how they do their work. Many of those same Millennials feel constrained in their job choices because of the debt burden hanging over them. These Millennials may feel obligated to work hard and put up with a lack of flexibility because they are worried about paying off their debts. For example, one Millennial we spoke with didn't like either the work he was doing or the hours (he was consistently working more than 55 hours a week), but he had significant student debts. He didn't quit because his monthly bills were so high as a result of his student debts, but he was always looking for a new job that would allow him to meet his financial obligations and have more of a life than he did in his current position.

Or how about the view of Millennials being needy we discussed in Chapter 2? One underlying cause of perceived neediness could be the unease the Millennials feel about their financial security. The daily tension created when people come to work concerned about their livelihoods and how they can provide for themselves and their families is real: it cannot be avoided by the Millennial generation any more easily than it has been by older generations.

Student Loan Numbers

According to one funding source, in 2012 in the United Kingdom, 907,200 students took out loans to pay their maintenance expenses associated with going to university, and 936,200 took out loans to pay their tuition.[21] As high as those numbers are, they most likely underrepresent the total because they are not a complete accounting of all loan sources. According to one source in Japan, in 2011, 1.29 million secondary school, university, and graduate students had taken out loans to finance their education.[22]

The Point

Millennials, like their older colleagues, have significant expenses they need to manage. For many, this includes student loans, along with standard living expenses. Being concerned about meeting basic financial needs reduces focus and productivity. Therefore, organizations benefit when Millennials are paid enough so they can focus on work rather than spend their time worrying about debts and bills.

Millennials Want to Do Well . . . Because They Are Concerned About Retirement

Though retirement is many years away for Millennials, many of them are thinking about it. The majority of Millennials in our study (55 percent) believe they will retire between the ages of 56 and 65. Though this is 20-30 years in the future for many of them, they are not sanguine about their retirement incomes: 84 percent of Millennials (and 89 percent of older employees) were concerned about whether they would be financially stable when they retired. The Millennials we spoke with were clear about the relationship between earnings now and security in retirement later. We were told,

> *The more I make now, the more I can save. The more I save early, the longer time the savings has to compound, and the more money I'll have for retirement. I can't rely on the government to pay for my retirement, so I have to make sure I have enough saved, independent of what they say they will pay me when I retire in about 30 years. The most likely way I will achieve that is if I save as much as I can now. But to do that, I need to make enough money.*

These concerns about financial stability in retirement are shared almost equally by most Millennials around the globe, with the exception of the Netherlands (see the data in Figure 3.9). In almost all countries, more than three-quarters of Millennials expressed this concern. There are some differences among the countries, with Mexico having the highest percentage of Millennials concerned

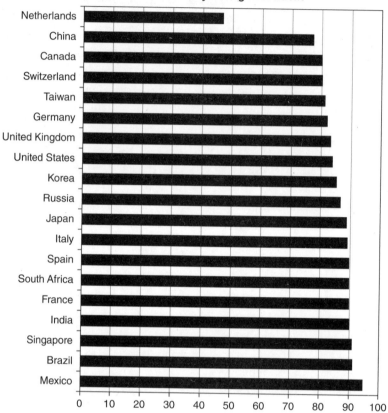

FIGURE 3.9: Percentage of Millennials Concerned About Their Financial Stability During Retirement

about this issue and the Netherlands the clear outlier at the other end of the spectrum. What is most striking is how similar the pattern is across countries, despite very different governmental approaches and generosity in public old age pension programs.

Despite their young age, Millennials see how their compensation contributes to their financial stability many years in the future. Some organizations realize this and make up for deficits in compensation with more substantial retirement packages. In the United States, Millennials who work for companies that provide a match of their retirement savings contributions appreciate the benefit of additional retirement savings.

The Point

Though retirement is many years in their future, Millennials around the world have significant concerns about their financial stability when they retire. Those fears cause them to focus on compensation and retirement savings. In addition to paying Millennials appropriately, organizations can look into alternative ways to help them save for retirement. Organizations that can add to their retirement savings at a low cost will reap the benefit of Millennials who are less likely to leave.

CONCLUSION: "SHARE MY VALUES" ISN'T JUST ABOUT DOING GOOD

As you can see, the evidence shows that Millennials want both to do good and to do well. While Millennials want an employer that shares their values and is a good corporate citizen, that isn't the only—or even the most important—value a Millennial holds dear. Any employer that wants to be aligned with Millennials' values needs to realize that compensation is likely to be the most important issue to them and behave accordingly.

Does this mean that Millennials are overly focused on compensation? The answer depends on how focused you believe a person should be. Millennials care about compensation just as much as the next person and want to work in organizations that share that concern. To Millennials, "sharing my values" is about the full range of values and includes the desire both to make a positive contribution to society and to be paid appropriately.

Given that Millennials want to both do good and do well, the following sections describe some actions you can take to work more effectively with them, whether you are a team member, a manager, or a leader.

How Different Are Millennials, Really?

Making the world a better place, being of service to society, and contributing to humanity are just as important to older generations as they are to Millennials. So is compensation. Employees older than Millennials may be less likely to talk about their compensation with coworkers, friends, or parents, but they do discuss their compensation with others (especially their spouses), look up information online, and have reference points for what others are paid. Like Millennials, they are concerned about paying bills, managing debt, and saving for retirement.

Recommendations for Working with Millennials as Team Members

Millennials want their work to make a contribution to the team, the organization, and society. Older team members can help them understand how the work contributes to the organization specifically and to the world generally. Older team members are more likely to see the connections clearly because of their greater experience. Understanding the connections will help Millennials be more enthusiastic about their jobs.

It is important to remember that each generation enters the workplace with a high ratio of idealism to practicality. When people are young and starting their careers, they don't really know how the world of work functions. Understanding the limitations as well as the potential of what can be accomplished in the workplace is a key part of the learning curve in Millennials' early working years.[23]

You may find yourself faced with team members who are very optimistic about how their employer can help make the world a better place. If that happens, the best thing to do as a team member is to help them understand how to act on their ideas without repressing their enthusiasm. Show them what has been done in the past in your organization and help them see how their ideas fit, from a practical perspective. Help them think through realistic scenarios of new initiatives that could be tried, and especially ways of approaching the right stakeholders to help make things happen.

Recommendations for Managing Millennials

1. Be a good corporate citizen—but don't expect them to think it makes up for deficiencies in compensation or opportunities.

Millennials want to be part of organizations that positively contribute to the world we all live in. Being a good corporate citizen can help your organization's image in the community and among Millennials. At the same time, don't believe that being a good corporate citizen is an acceptable substitute for a healthy paycheck or opportunities for development and advancement. It is not.

Therefore, managers and leaders should focus on employees' needs both to do good and to be paid appropriately. Take the time and effort to figure out—ideally, with the employees' help and input—where your organization can do a better job of making a positive contribution to society. But also take the time and effort to ensure that compensation is set right so that employees are appropriately rewarded for their hard work and contributions to the organization.

2. Enable them to engage in the world outside the office, whether through volunteering, global assignments, or in other ways.

Millennials want to engage in the world outside the office. Give them as much opportunity to integrate their personal interests and goals into their jobs as is appropriate without disrupting the work flow. For some, this might mean taking advantage of company-sponsored opportunities to volunteer in the local community. For others, it might mean being able to see a different part of the world through a work assignment. There is no one-size-fits-all solution, and you don't have to bend over backward to give everyone his or her preferred outlet. But the more opportunities you can offer for employees to do what they are interested in at work, the greater the positive response you are likely to get from them.

Therefore, managers should, as much as possible, provide opportunities for employees to engage with the world outside the office. Though you may be aware of all the options, your employees are unlikely to be as familiar with the possibilities. They also might be unsure of how supportive you are of them getting involved beyond their core job responsibilities. If employees don't feel they have your explicit approval and encouragement to get involved in company-sponsored community activities, they might hesitate to take part. They may think that even if an opportunity is made available, they should take advantage of it only if it doesn't affect their primary job duties. Therefore, be clear on what you think is valuable for them to do, and help them think through how they will meet their current obligations while also taking advantage of opportunities.

The role you can play in helping facilitate assignments abroad is even larger. Though many Millennials yearn for the chance to have a posting in a different country, they often don't know much about the actual opportunities. They need your help to understand the options and the implications of taking the assignment, as well as how to assess their expectations against the reality of what is possible. After all, these assignments aren't always as glamorous as they might appear, and it is critical that Millennials understand that before they take them on.

3. Pay them what they are worth and realize that they know what standard compensation is—so don't try to hide pay information from them.

Compensation matters to all employees— period. Millennials are no exception. Even if your company is a good corporate citizen and provides a lot of opportunities to engage in the world outside the office, you still have to treat employees right when it comes to pay.

Don't think you will succeed in hiding substandard compensation. Millennials have more means than ever to figure out how much they are worth in the labor market. They freely share information about their compensation with others and seek out information that is readily available online. Underpay or mislead them about compensation at your own peril.

Watch out for signs that employees might be unhappy with their compensation. You may not have much control over how much your people are paid, but you are the first one who is likely to notice when things are amiss. Dissatisfaction with compensation doesn't always show up immediately as complaints about paychecks.

Instead, their productivity might fall off, they might seem less engaged, or they might be visibly unhappy. These are all signs that they are "checking out" while continuing to come to work every day.

HR knows that most managers want their people paid more, especially if the increase in compensation won't come out of their own budget. But it can be difficult for HR to stay current with the shifting external labor market for employee skills. So it's up to you to help keep an eye open for signs that pay is falling behind and let HR know when you see anything that suggests a big gap. Rest assured, your employees will notice your attempts on their behalf as much as they will be aware of being underpaid.

4. Recognize and help them manage the real financial pressures they are under by providing them with good options.

Millennials are concerned about the financial pressures they face in their lives. Whether it's dealing with high student debt, struggling to afford a mortgage for expensive housing, or working hard to support a reasonable standard of living, they understand their position all too well. Many are worried about retirement and whether their standard of living and quality of life will exceed that of their parents. The more you can help them deal with their financial challenges through realistic career planning and developmental opportunities so they can advance and make more money, the more grateful they will be to you and the organization.

Keep an eye out for signs of financial stress. This is the companion piece to making sure employees are paid appropriately. Even when pay is in line with the external labor market for their skills, employees can still feel enormous pressure from not making enough money to manage their lives and plan for the future. It is not your job as their manager to solve their financial problems, especially if pay has been set appropriately. But that doesn't diminish the potential negative impact on engagement and morale if your people feel stressed by financial issues outside work.

If you know the details of why your employees are stressed financially, you can offer words of encouragement and career advice on how to succeed in the long run. And even if you don't know the details, being compassionate if you suspect they have financial issues going on outside work can go a long way. You can help boost their morale and keep them engaged and productive at work because they know you care about them as people, not just as cogs in the organizational machine. That matters to all staff.

Five Points to Remember

1. Millennials want to contribute to their community.
2. Millennials want their work to be meaningful and interesting—more than just a job that pays the bills.
3. Millennials don't believe they should have to accept substantially lower pay just because their organization contributes to the community.
4. Millennials struggle with financial issues that affect their career and job choices.
5. Millennials will find out how much they should be paid and will tell you about it even if you don't want them to.

Who Millennials Are and What They Want

Millennials:
- Want to make a contribution to the community
- Want to work for a socially responsible organization
- Think globally
- Believe doing good isn't more important than doing well
- Are motivated to work and want to be paid well for it
- Are concerned about paying their bills and debt
- Are concerned about retirement
- Believe compensation reflects how much their organization values them

CHAPTER 4

HIGH TECH *AND* HIGH TOUCH

Eric is a Millennial working on a team in a large professional services firm. He really enjoys hanging out with his team and will take every opportunity to go out with team members after work. He loves technology, wears headphones all the time so he can listen to music or podcasts while he is working, is always carrying around the newest devices and talking about the latest features, and instant messages (IMs) people sitting 10 feet away from him just because it's fun. One day, he had finished his assigned work by midafternoon, so he decided to watch a show on his phone to relax. He figured he was done with his work early, so he could kick back and take a break. He was partway through his show when his boss appeared behind him and asked him what he was doing. He explained that he was watching a show to take a break since he was finished with his work. His boss took a deep breath (to calm down) and then explained that (1) watching shows at work wasn't allowed; and (2) if he had finished his work, he should go ask members of his team whether he could help them. He is part of the team, after all. Eric hadn't thought of it. In his mind, when he finished his own work, he was done. Once the issue was pointed out to him, he was concerned that his team members would think badly of him because he didn't think to help them. He immediately got up and went around helping people—and bought the first round of drinks after work.

Eric loves technology, and it is what he defaults to when looking for something to do. But he also cares a great deal about the people he works with. Do Millennials love technology? Yes. They want their new tech devices and the latest apps. They want to do most of their communication electronically because it is more efficient. But are they happy to have technology replace human contact? No. The people they work with are critically important to them and their experience at work.

MILLENNIALS LOVE TECHNOLOGY AND WANT ALL THE TECH TOYS THEY CAN GET, RIGHT?

Would I like it if they'd give us iPads to use when we came to work here? Absolutely!

—Millennial

Yes, Millennials love their tech toys. They would prefer to have whatever is newest. They want the latest hardware and software. According to a 2010 report on Millennials by the Pew Research Center, they are more likely to have a social network profile, to have posted a video of themselves, to use Twitter, and to send text messages than are older generations.[1] That same 2010 report said that 74 percent of Millennials believe that new technology makes life easier.[2]

Why do Millennials love tech so much? They are comfortable with it. They have grown up with technology, starting at an earlier age than any previous generation. They make and maintain friendships through technology. They gain status within their own social groups as a result of having the newest and best tech toys. Their proficiency with technology provides them with status at work (how many times have you seen older staff ask someone in their twenties for help with a computer?). But we believe the biggest reason Millennials love technology at work is because it reduces drudgery and saves them time.

Millennials Are High Tech . . . They Think Technology Reduces Drudgery and Saves Time

Recall from Chapter 1 that Millennials don't like boring work. In part, they love technology because it reduces the laborious, uninteresting work they dislike so much. According to a 2010 report by the Pew Research Center, half of Millennials believe that new technology allows people to use their time more efficiently.[3] Many Millennials believe that there is a tech solution for pretty much everything that they don't want to do.

Joke

How many Millennials does it take to change a lightbulb?
Unclear—they're still looking for an app for that.

In some cases, what Millennials don't realize is that their tech "solution" is actually shifting the workload to others. So the high-tech solution that causes *them* less work because they already know how to use the system causes more work for those who don't know the system or have to implement the system.

Recall the story from Chapter 1 about Millennials and their older bosses who disagree about the use of "track changes" in electronic documents. Millennials told us that they would create a report in Microsoft Word and send it to the appropriate boss for review. Rather than reviewing it onscreen and sending an electronic document back to the Millennial with tracked changes and notes, the boss would instead hand the Millennial a paper copy with notes written in the margins. Getting all the edits incorporated often took multiple iterations, which the Millennials thought was unnecessarily time consuming.

The Millennials said this process used them as transcribers. They are capable of doing the work, but it is a waste of their time (and organizational resources) when the initial reviewers could have typed the changes themselves. Also, it's boring to transcribe what someone else has written. It is more interesting to work with edits made in an electronic file and make changes on top of those to improve the final product.

This manual process really does take a lot of time. Why does it happen? When we spoke with the older people who were making the notes on paper, they told us they did it this way because they don't like using track changes. They said that they understood it would save the Millennials time if they put their notes in track changes, but they are used to making notes on physical pages so it is faster for them. They also find track changes confusing and more difficult to use.

Saving Millennials' time or helping them avoid boring work was not a priority for the bosses. Frankly, their bosses' time is (financially) worth many times what the typical Millennial's time is worth to the organization. So if the bosses' time is saved by making notes on paper, that is what is going to happen. Both parties prefer the method that saves them the most time and makes their work experience the most pleasant. And as typically happens in organizations, the people with the most clout get to make the rules, and others follow them.

If you realize Millennials are choosing the least laborious route *for them* to get something done, then their automatic use of technology will make more sense. They send an e-mail, instant message, or text, depending on what is most efficient for them to use at the moment. And when we say most efficient, we mean "do what needs to be done quickly." Remember, they dislike their time being wasted by others. (It is OK if they choose to waste it themselves because that is their choice and not something imposed on them.)

This is true even when they are volunteering.[4] In a survey of volunteers by Achieve, 69 percent said that their biggest pet peeve when volunteering was having their time wasted, and 47 percent were bothered that they had to attend training sessions in person that could have been done equally well online and asynchronously.[5]

Millennials like to do things in a way that is most efficient for them and best meets their needs, which typically involves technology. But this isn't unique to Millennials; people of all generations use the method that is easiest for them. A client may prefer to receive a phone call rather than an e-mail, but the Millennial employee may not realize this and will send an e-mail because that method is more efficient for the Millennial. Similarly, Millennials' bosses may provide them with critical information electronically, such as feedback about their performance or their compensation, when Millennials would prefer to receive that information face-to-face (more on this later).

So yes, Millennials are high tech. They gravitate toward work that includes technology because tech is both intrinsically interesting to them and faster and easier for them to use.

The Point

Millennials like technology and want to use technology to reduce unnecessary drudgery at work. Managers can work with Millennials to find a solution to avoid the boring work (if such a solution exists). Managers need to explain the problem to Millennials if their preferred solution simply shifts the uninteresting work to other employees. Organizations and all employees will benefit if solutions can be found that reduce unnecessary drudgery overall.

Millennials Are High Tech . . . They Maintain Friendships Through Cyberspace

Perhaps one of the most hyperbolic stereotypes about the Millennial generation is that they are so connected to the Internet and social networking that they do almost all of their socializing that way. That of course is not true—most see their friends as well as texting, emailing and IMing them, rather than only interacting with them virtually. But a 2010 study by the Pew Research Center reported that a majority of Millennials in the United States[6] believe that new technology helps people stay closer to their friends and family.[7]

Millennials use a variety of methods to connect with friends, and as much as they like to spend time with friends face-to-face, they are also likely to describe people they only interact with virtually as friends. With the increase in global mobility, people are increasingly likely to live far away from their friends and family. Many of the Millennials we spoke with around the world said that keeping in touch with friends digitally was the only way they could maintain contact with many of them. It isn't just that people are busy; it is also because they no longer live near their friends.

We were told that after university, many of their friends moved to different places for work and family reasons, so if they wanted to remain close to these people, they had to use electronic methods. A few Millennials commented that technology is especially helpful for maintaining relationships with friends they had made over-seas. Many had spent a semester or term abroad and had made friendships they wanted to maintain when they moved back to their home countries.

Millennials have adapted to this reality by relying on technology-mediated ways to maintain relationships with their large friend networks. Facebook, e-mail, instant messaging, Instagram, and Skype help them keep up with friends who are far away. Millennials say they are more likely to use phone, e-mail, and text messaging for connecting with friends they don't see very often (see Figure 4.1).

Millennials report maintaining some social relationships almost exclusively through cyberspace. Twenty-nine percent say that they have friends they have met through the web whom they haven't met in person, while 42 percent of Millennials say that they have friends they interact with only in cyberspace. Figure 4.2 shows what that looks like for Millennials around the world. We see that it is not uncommon for Millennials to have at least one friend with whom they interact exclusively through cyberspace; the percentage varies

FIGURE 4.1: Percentage Who Choose to Use Each Method of Communication to Maintain Relationships with Friends They Don't See Very Often

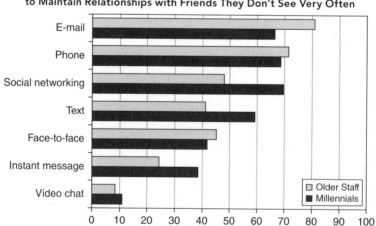

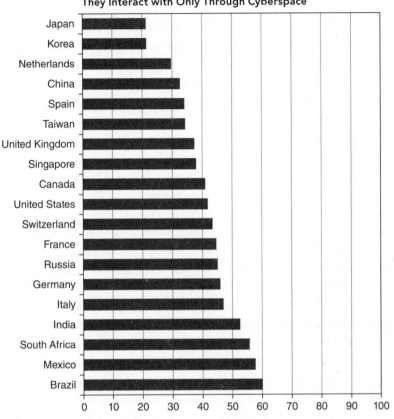

FIGURE 4.2: Percentage of Millennials with Friends
They Interact with Only Through Cyberspace

widely from country to country. Korea and Japan have among the lowest rates, while Brazil, Mexico, South Africa, and India have the highest. North America and Europe are in the middle.

While some claim Millennials aren't connected with each other because they spend their time focused on their electronic devices, our interviews with Millennials indicate that they are often interacting with others while buried in their phones. It isn't the platform they use to connect, but the fact that they are connected that is important. For them, face-to-face time isn't the only way to have a meaningful connection with another person. Many of them have learned how to maintain relationships electronically, which can increase rather than decrease their circle of friends—all appearances to the contrary!

The Point

Millennials are used to living far away from people they care about, and many have become comfortable maintaining relationships purely though cyberspace. This capacity will be an advantage to them in the long term, as organizations continue to become more dispersed. Organizations can leverage Millennials' ability to manage and maintain relationships through cyberspace by engaging in practices such as assigning them to work on geographically dispersed teams.

Millennials Are High Tech . . . They Rely on Technology Too Much!

In our interviews around the globe, we heard repeatedly how technologically advanced the Millennials are. In many cases, the implication was that they relied on technology too much. For example, we were told stories of

- Millennials who chose to IM people in the same room rather than asking a question out loud.
- Millennials who e-mailed clients rather than calling them on the phone.
- Millennials who asked long, involved questions over e-mail rather than walking to an office a few doors away.
- Millennials who continued to respond by electronic means to someone who was clearly confused rather than speaking with the other person, when doing so would have quickly taken care of the problem.

It is important to note that the older generations (primarily Generation X) also make extensive use of technology, including overuse at times. (How many times have you rolled your eyes at a really long e-mail communicating something that should have been handled in person or by phone that was sent by someone older than a Millennial?) The difference between the generations shows up more in the *types* of technology used, especially in their social relationships.[8]

Millennials are much more likely to use newer technology, such as social networking, texting, and instant messaging, to maintain relationships with friends they don't see very often (see Figure 4.1). People from older generations are more likely to use e-mail and, in fact, use e-mail more often than face-to-face communication or even talking on the phone.

We don't think the differences in Figure 4.1 indicate that older generations are technology-phobic. The older generation entered adulthood at a time when e-mail was the brand-new sexy technology that they embraced more quickly than their elders. They established lifelong friendships and patterns of interacting with their generational peers that centered on e-mail, and those patterns persist to today. It will be interesting to see if the pattern holds over time, with Millennials imprinting on the forms of technology they used in their twenties and being unwilling to switch when a newer technology comes along.

The differences in Figure 4.1 also provide another explanation for tensions among the generations about technology usage in the workplace. Millennials are clearly comfortable using multiple types of technology to maintain social relationships outside of work, so they are going to be more inclined to use—or even demand the use of—those same technologies in their work relationships. Older generations are much more comfortable with e-mail and the phone, and are less likely to use social networks, text messaging, and instant messaging. So they may be slower to embrace those technologies at work which they don't see as improvements, instead defaulting to their preferred ones, while Millennials continue to push for their preferred technologies.

The Point

Millennials rely on technology about as much as their older peers do, but the technologies they rely on may be different. Millennials often prefer to use newer tech systems that are less likely to be used commonly across the organization. If this tendency affects their ability to communicate effectively, help them understand and use the dominant technology so they can be successful. Leverage Millennials' interest in technology systems to identify new communication methods that may improve efficiency for all.

TECH IS GREAT, BUT CONNECTION MATTERS JUST AS MUCH TO MILLENNIALS

While Millennials want to make effective use of their time and use the technology they prefer, they clearly value connecting with people, and they realize that not all information is best communicated through an electronic medium. For Millennials, connections at work with friends, their teams, and their supervisors are critical to how they feel about work.

Millennials Are High Touch . . . They Generally Prefer Face-to-Face Communication

One of the complaints we have often heard about Millennials is that they don't understand the importance of nonverbal communication in effectively understanding and communicating with others. We heard countless stories about Millennials who chose to communicate electronically when they should have chosen to speak with the person face-to-face. This behavior was explained to us as evidence of Millennials' preference for electronic rather than in-person communication. Our data suggest that this type of behavior is *not* an indication that Millennials prefer electronic communication. We think this happens because Millennials perceive these communications to be less critical and thus acceptable to occur electronically.

We find that Millennials actually prefer face-to-face communication to other forms. In our interviews, Millennials were clearly aware that they can have greater influence and improve the perception of themselves more through face-to-face interaction than through technology-mediated communication. The data in Table 4.1 clearly show that they act on this knowledge by focusing first and foremost on face-to-face communication with colleagues at all levels of the organization.

Whether they are communicating with colleagues at lower, equal, or higher levels, approximately three-quarters of Millennials prefer face-to-face communication for each group as their first choice. During our interviews and focus groups, it was apparent that face-to-face was their preference, but they didn't always communicate that way. We were told that when they think about how to communicate with others, they are balancing importance and expediency. If face-to-face communication will take substantially more effort than electronic, Millennials are likely to make a calculation about whether the importance of the communication merits the additional effort.

TABLE 4.1 How Millennials Prefer to Communicate with Colleagues

MILLENNIALS' FIRST CHOICE OF COMMUNICATION	LOWER-LEVEL COLLEAGUES	SAME-LEVEL COLLEAGUES	HIGHER-LEVEL COLLEAGUES
Face-to-face	78%	79%	75%
Phone	7%	5%	6%
E-mail	9%	5%	16%
IM	6%	10%	3%
Text	0%	0%	0%
Social networking site	0%	0%	0%
Video chat	0%	0%	0%

For example, if it is as easy to have the communication face-to-face as electronically, Millennials might default to speaking with someone face-to-face regardless of what the subject matter is.

But if communicating face-to-face requires significant effort on the part of the Millennials, they might go to the trouble only if they consider the information or conversation to be particularly important to them (not necessarily taking the importance of the conversation to the other party into consideration).

Millennials will go to the trouble of having a face-to-face conversation when receiving *performance evaluation feedback*. It is likely that most Millennials understand they can get more information about their performance that they can use to improve their position within the organization if they can see the nonverbal behaviors of the person providing the feedback. Technology-mediated forms of communication don't provide non-verbal cues the way face-to-face communication does. They may also realize that they have a greater advantage in a face-to-face encounter because they can have more influence on the perception of the person if they are speaking face-to-face.

Millennials prefer receiving performance evaluation feedback in the following ways:

- Face-to-face: 92 percent
- E-mail: 5 percent
- Phone: 2 percent
- IM: 1 percent
- Text: 0 percent
- Social networking site: 0 percent
- Video chat: 0 percent

When talking about *their career plans or progress*, Millennials overwhelmingly want the communication to happen face-to-face. It is likely that most Millennials understand that they have greater influence over the outcome of career planning meetings if they are held face-to-face. It is more difficult to refuse requests from someone face-to-face than it is at a distance. If an individual is making a substantial request, it is more strategic to make that request in person than through some form of technology-mediated communication. Clearly, Millennials see the importance of face-to-face communication when addressing career issues.

Millennials prefer talking about their career plans and performance in the following ways:

- Face-to-face: 95 percent
- E-mail: 3 percent
- Phone: 2 percent
- IM: 0 percent
- Text: 0 percent
- Social networking site: 0 percent
- Video chat: 0 percent

When discussing *their compensation*, as with receiving feedback and discussing career plans, most Millennials prefer that the conversations take place face-to-face. However, unlike feedback on performance and conversations about their career, Millennials are more willing to communicate over e-mail when their compensation is the topic. It is possible this is because conversations about compensation are often not as open to influence as are conversations about feedback or career planning, so receiving the information over e-mail is perceived as less of a disadvantage.

Millennials prefer discussing their compensation in the following ways:

- Face-to-face: 79 percent
- E-mail: 17 percent
- Phone: 4 percent
- IM: 0 percent
- Text: 0 percent
- Social networking site: 0 percent
- Video chat: 0 percent

When the conversation is about something Millennials believe is important to them (their performance, their career, or their compensation), they really want the conversation to happen face-to-face. When the conversation is about something someone else thinks is critical, Millennials still believe that it should be done face-to-face, but not as overwhelmingly.

Newfangled Technology and Evolving "Proper" Communication Methods

Even though the vast majority of Millennials say they prefer face-to-face interaction for communicating with clients and customers, we ran into quite a few instances in which the general perception of Millennials is that they are much too quick to default to technology for client or customer communication. The typical lament was, "I don't understand why they are so quick to send an e-mail or even a text message when it would be so much more professional to pick up the phone or even go to the client in person."

Our data show that many Millennials opt first for communication methods that are not face-to-face for conversations with customers, supervisors, and colleagues. But that isn't necessarily wrong. For instance, if they are choosing phone or e-mail first and face-to-face interactions second, that could be entirely appropriate: they leave a voice mail or send e-mail first, and then follow up face-to-face.

To see if that is what is going on, we looked at both the first and second choices for communicating with customers, supervisors, and colleagues (see Table 4.2). The vast majority (about 85 percent) of Millennials use face-to-face communication for either their first or second choice across a wide range of work communications.

TABLE 4.2 Percentage of Millennials Choosing Face-to-Face as Either Their First or Second Choice for Communicating

With clients or customers	84%
With colleagues at lower levels	85%
With colleagues at higher levels	84%
With colleagues at the same level	87%
To receive their performance feedback	96%
To discuss their career plan progress	97%
To discuss their compensation	87%

While everyone, including Millennials, agrees that face-to-face communication is the most personal, the world doesn't stand still, certainly when it comes to how technology is used at work. Many Millennials are completely comfortable conducting more types of communication using technology, such as texting, social networking, and instant messaging. As their numbers grow in the workforce and as they ascend to higher- and higher-level roles in the organization and interact more with suppliers and customers, some of the norms of what had been considered to be "proper" business communication in the past are likely to change.

Consider the experience a couple of parents had with their Millennial daughter. The parents would constantly harp on their daughter to pick up the phone to call her friends rather than do everything via text messages. The daughter resisted their pleas (even though she admitted they had a point—sometimes) and insisted on using text messaging as the primary means of communicating with her friends. One day when they were riding in the car together, she piped up, "You know, when I have kids, I'm probably going say to them, 'Why don't you just text your friends?'" She realized that the generation following hers would have some newfangled technology that would be just as foreign to her as texting was to her parents and that she would have concerns largely similar to those of her parents, albeit about a different technology.

We do not believe, as some in the past have predicted with prior technology innovations, that in-person communication will ever "die"—there will always be a need for in-person communication for many critical business issues (as well as critical social issues). Yet just as e-mail took the place of some types of in-person and telephone-based communication when it was fully adopted by businesses, a similar evolution is bound to happen for technologies to come. Looking forward 20 years from now, when Millennials will occupy most middle and senior management roles, we fully expect large parts, but not the overwhelming majority, of business communication to take place over these new technologies.

WORKING DAZE © 2009 John Zakour and Scott Roberts. Reprinted by permission of UNIVERSAL UCLICK for UFS. All rights reserved.

Given that the majority of Millennials prefer face-to-face communication, why does the stereotype persist that Millennials prefer to communicate electronically? Perhaps it is because people see them buried in their computers, tablets, and phones so much of the time and assume that their preference is to communicate that way. Everyone can think of one or two examples of a time a Millennial should have communicated in person and didn't, but people don't necessarily remember the times an older employee did the same. Our results demonstrate how critical personal connections are to Millennials, regardless of how much time they spend with their eyes focused on one screen or another.

The Point

While Millennials may like technology, they prioritize face-to-face communication for conversations they perceive as important. Managers need to do their best to have face-to-face conversations when talking with Millennials about information that is important to them (e.g., about compensation, career, or performance). Managers can also help Millennials figure out how to identify what information is important to others so they can have conversations on those topics face-to-face as well.

Millennials Are High Touch . . . Their Community at Work Matters a Lot to Them

Though they love technology, Millennials are definitely high touch. While technology is important, the human aspect of work is even more important. If they don't feel emotionally connected to their workplace either through friends or team members or their boss, they are a flight risk. Millennials who don't have an emotional connection to their organization will seek it elsewhere. At work, they want friends, teams they feel friendly with, a boss who cares about them, and an organization of which they feel part.

Friends at Work

Friends are critical to Millennials, both at home and at work. Ninety-eight percent of Millennials say that developing close ties with coworkers is important to them. In fact, having friends and close coworkers at work is so important that it is strongly related to how committed a Millennial feels to the organization. Why? Our guess is that it has to do with the current life stage of the majority of Millennials. Most of the Millennials in our sample haven't started families, and many are more likely to rely on their friends than a spouse. At this point in their lives, friends simply loom larger, as they did for Baby Boomers and Gen Xers at the same life stage.

This was clear to us during our interviews. We heard from Millennials all over the world about how important their friends at work were to them. They talked about the evenings out after a long week, sports teams they played on, weekend parties, and double dates. Many told us that having the chance to spend time with their friends at work makes work a place they wanted to be—and a place they didn't mind spending 12 or so hours a day during the week.

Given how important friends at work are to Millennials, it is good news that a majority of Millennials feel that they have friends there. Sixty-six percent say they have formed strong friendships at work, and 60 percent say they can confide in people at work, which means that a majority have relationships at work that help make the workplace a place they want to be (the percentages are similar for older generations).

One way Millennials cultivate friendships with others at work is through socializing outside of office hours. About one in five say that they socialize with people from work every week, and about two in five say that they socialize with people from work a couple of times a month or every month.

While only one-fifth of Millennials may socialize with friends from work outside the workplace every week, their friends at work are definitely a big draw for them. Fifty-four percent say that being able to see their coworkers is one of the reasons they look forward to their job. When Millennials don't have coworkers they like or feel they have a good working relationship with, they become dissatisfied and are likely to want to leave the group or the organization.

Millennials tend to socialize with people at their level more than they do with people above or below them within the organizational hierarchy. Eighty-nine percent say they get together with people at the same job level, while 61 percent say they socialize with people above their level in the organization, and slightly fewer[9] say that they socialize with people below their organizational level. Older employees report seeing their coworkers less frequently outside of work than do Millennials but are just as likely to report having good friends at work and seeing these coworkers as a primary reason they look forward to going to work.

In addition to socializing outside of work, three-quarters of Millennials report that they contact coworker friends through either internal or external social networking sites. In all countries except Japan, more than 60 percent of Millennials contact their coworkers using internal or external social networking sites (see Figure 4.3). And for 64 percent of those, some contact among coworkers is taking place *outside of corporate systems*. This is true for Millennials at all levels in the organization. This is positive because it shows how robust the relationships are. But make sure that employees know what information can be talked about outside of workplace systems, and what cannot, even among friends.

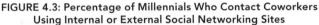

FIGURE 4.3: Percentage of Millennials Who Contact Coworkers Using Internal or External Social Networking Sites

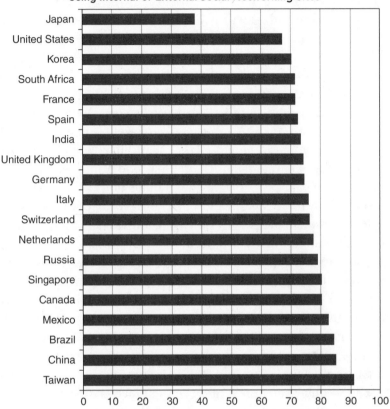

The Point

Millennials' connections with friends are critical to their lives in general and to their experience at work in particular. Even if their interaction is only virtual, having friends at work matters to Millennials because it makes work a place they want to be. They aren't happy simply playing on devices; they want other people to connect with—and perhaps play on the devices with them! Organizations benefit when their employees develop workplace friendships. While organizations can't assign friends as they can mentors, they can facilitate the development of friendships through workplace teams, events, and interest groups.

Connecting with Their Team

A crucial part of Millennials' experience at work is the team they work on. For organizations, teamwork is a core part of the work design—without it, many critical tasks would never be accomplished efficiently and effectively. The good news is that Millennials see high value in working on teams, not just because it enables the work, but because of the social interactions it provides.

Many Millennials talked about how they were willing to work late to make sure their team's goals were met. Some talked about voluntarily staying to support other team members who hadn't finished their work and going to get food for hungry members of their teams who couldn't leave. Many said that they wouldn't feel connected to their organization if it weren't for the teams they were on. To them, the team is the organization, in a tangible way.

Millennials' desire to be part of a team at work is strong across all the countries in our data. Except for in Korea, more than 60 percent of Millennials, and more than 80 percent in some, would rather work as part of a group than work alone (see Figure 4.4). Even in the United States, where everyone is supposed to be very individually oriented, more than 70 percent of Millennials would rather work as part of a group.

As work within organizations becomes more structured around teams, Millennials find themselves spending more time in team environments and relying on the members of their teams. Though the membership of a team changes as work shifts and projects come and go, the support Millennials perceive from their teams is an important part of their community at work. Almost three-quarters of Millennials[10] (and about as many older staff)[11] say that their teams have a great deal of personal meaning to them.

Happily, a majority of Millennials feel connected to the teams they work on:

- 64 percent say they feel as if they are an important member of their teams.
- 57 percent say that they have a strong sense of belonging to their teams.
- 59 percent say that colleagues on their teams really care about their well-being.

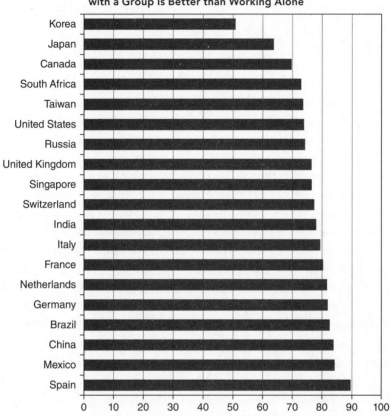

FIGURE 4.4: Percentage of Millennials Who Say Working
with a Group Is Better than Working Alone

This means that a majority of Millennials have a positive relationship with their teams, which is good because their membership in a team is so important to them.

Millennials are dedicated team members and strongly believe in working in team environments. While Millennials want control and autonomy, three-quarters[12] say that they prefer working with a group to working alone. Even when things aren't going well, four out of five believe they should stay with the group and help rather than work alone.

Millennials' behavior demonstrates how important their teams are to them. Remember the story about Eric at the beginning of the chapter? Though he was watching a show on his phone, as soon as it was pointed out that he was letting his team down, he stopped watching and started helping out his team members. Helping team members is common for Millennials: about 80 percent report that they volunteer to do things for their teams, help others on their teams with their responsibilities, and get involved beyond their job responsibilities to benefit their teams. Millennials believe that their attitude toward their teams is reciprocated: about 80 percent say that colleagues on their teams will help them when they have a problem and are willing to help them if they need a special favor.

The Point

Millennials' teams really matter to their experience at work. The good news is that the majority of Millennials are pretty happy with the teams they are on: they feel they can trust the members of the team, they say the team cares about them personally, and they are willing to go beyond their specific job responsibilities to help people on their team. This is particularly positive because we have found that feeling part of a team affects Millennials' organizational commitment, job satisfaction, and intention to remain with the organization. Organizations benefit when they provide environments for Millennials that allow them to work with others on teams so they can develop the community at work that they need.

Having a Boss They Connect With

Their relationships with their bosses are just as important to Millennials as their relationships with their friends at work or the teams of which they are a part.

Millennials have very specific ideas about what makes a good boss or leader. They believe that good leaders are considerate, kind, and willing to help others; they care about others and want to get to know the people they work with and form relationships with them. Millennials expect leaders to help members of their teams and encourage teamwork and collaborative behavior. They also believe that good leaders inspire and motivate others (see Appendix 4.1). While many Millennials may not have leaders that live up to their expectations of what a good leader is, the good news is that a majority believe that their managers care about their well-being[13] and are generally supportive.[14]

The Need to Be Appreciated

During our interviews, one common refrain we heard from everyone (Millennials, older staff, and managers) is that a large percentage of Millennials say they don't feel appreciated at work. (Incidentally, the older people we spoke with said they didn't feel appreciated either, so this feeling is common.) However, a majority (58 percent of Millennials and 61 percent of their older peers) say that they *do* feel appreciated at work.

While that is a majority, about 40 percent—and slightly more Millennials than older workers—don't feel appreciated at work. In other words, many believe their workplace is consistent with the saying, "Doing a good job around here is like wetting your pants in a dark suit. It gives you a nice warm feeling, but nobody notices."[15]

One woman we interviewed talked specifically about how she didn't feel appreciated. She received strong performance appraisals and pay increases, but she said she never felt as if her boss actually appreciated her work. She said she received a perfunctory performance review where she was told that her performance was excellent, but that was it. No specifics about what she had done well, no suggestions for how she could improve, and no simple statement about how much he appreciated the work she did for the organization. When last we spoke, she was trying to get transferred to another boss who had a better reputation for appreciating staff.

Millennials want to feel appreciated, just as everyone else does. And if they don't feel appreciated where they are, they'll see where they can go to feel appreciated.

The bad news is that a large minority of Millennials do not think that their bosses care about their well-being, and more than a quarter[16] don't feel that their supervisors are supportive. Worse, one in five say that their managers show little concern for them and don't appreciate it when they put in extra effort. That means that 20 to 40 percent of Millennials don't feel as if their managers are meeting their needs for connection and community.

It is critical for organizations to pay attention to the discrepancy between what Millennials want and what they are experiencing. While Millennials may like their tech toys, it is their relationships, such as those with their bosses, that make or break their experience at work. Regardless of the actual levels of support, the discrepancy between what Millennials believe supervisors should do and what supervisors actually do has a profound impact on organizational commitment and engagement.

The Point

Millennials' connections with their supervisors have a large impact on how they feel about their workplace, as they do for all employees. Make sure that supervisors recognize the importance of connection and do what they can to address their employees' needs. Doing so will help improve how employees feel about the entire organization.

Feeling Connected with the Organization as a Whole

In addition to having friends, feeling part of a team, and having a boss they like and trust, Millennials want to feel connected to their organization as a whole. For Millennials, some of that connection comes from shared values (see Chapter 3) and some from feeling that their organization cares about them.

A majority of Millennials feel their organization cares about their general satisfaction at work,[17] and more than two-thirds believe that their organization values their contribution to its well-being.[18] In 2013, Achieve published a study of Millennials that found that "more than half (53 percent) of respondents said having their passions and talents recognized and addressed is their top reason for remaining at their current company."[19]

One Millennial we spoke with, who worked for a global company, talked about how he didn't identify just with the local office he worked in; he felt as if he were part of the larger global community within the organization. He said he participated in online groups with other employees from all over the world who were interested in the same subject (in this case, rugby). Beyond his immediate friends, teammates, and boss, the organization as a large global entity held real meaning for him because he felt it supported him and his interests. Between the global affinity groups and the opportunity to work with people all over the world (either virtually or through possible global assignments), he felt the organization as a whole was an important part of his work experience.

Feeling that connection to the larger community at work is important, for it benefits both the Millennial and the organization. The old saying that people don't leave organizations, they leave their bosses, is just as true for Millennials as it is for older workers. But that too-simple statement leaves out the critical connection to people other than the immediate supervisor.

Even Millennials don't expect nirvana at work, so they aren't going to stampede for the door just because their bosses are less than perfect. And a large part of what keeps them from leaving is their connection to the larger organization. That includes relationships with their immediate team members, friendships throughout the organization, mentors who can help guide them in their careers, and so on.

Connection with the organization as a whole is important because it also represents future opportunities. The prospect of working for other bosses and having experiences that enable professional and personal growth is all part of the package that comes with working for an organization. Commitment to the organization as a whole is built on the foundation of these multifaceted relationships that together define the Millennials' experience at work.

The Point
The organization itself is an important part of Millennials' experience of the workplace. An organization's values, norms, and culture are part of the foundation that defines employees' daily work experiences. Supervisors play an important role in employees' experiences at work, but they are only one among many individuals and groups that make up each person's experience of the larger organization. Leaders in organizations need to provide employees with opportunities to connect with others beyond their immediate supervisor.

Conclusion: Millennials Like Technology, But People Are Just as Important to Them

As you can see, the evidence shows that Millennials are high tech, but they also are high touch. Just because Millennials spend so much time attached to one tech toy or another (literally 24/7 for some, with the wearable technology currently available), that doesn't mean people aren't essential to their experience of life in general and of work in particular. People are important. Feeling like they have a community at work is a determining factor in employees' commitment to their organization, job satisfaction, engagement, and retention. In other words, when Millennials don't have a tech toy, they may be slightly annoyed; when they don't have a community, they look for a place to go that will give them one.

Given that Millennials are simultaneously high tech and high touch, the following sections describe some actions you can take to work more effectively with them, whether you are a team member, a manager, or a leader.

Recommendations for Working with Millennials as Team Members

As team members, Millennials want to use the most efficient means possible to get their work done. For them, that is likely to be a technological solution. While this tendency may be frustrating, it also might end up saving time. Think about it—if someone can figure out a way to do the work more efficiently and just as accurately, that saves you time and lets you apply your skills to work that is more interesting and valuable for the organization.

While Millennials believe technology is their friend, in some cases it is a crutch. You can show them how to stop relying on it so much. We have heard many stories where Millennials defaulted to sending an e-mail that resulted in unnecessary confusion and ruffled feathers. You can help Millennials learn when a phone call or face-to-face conversation would be more effective and efficient than technology-mediated communication. You can do this by modeling the behavior and explaining why you made one choice or the other, and by coaching them directly. This will help Millennials become more savvy organizational citizens, and it will help save you from some of those endless (and unnecessary) e-mail exchanges!

How Different Are Millennials, Really?

While people talk about Millennials doing everything electronically, older generations are as likely as Millennials to interact with people through cyberspace[20] or to have friends they have met through the web whom they haven't met in person.[21] Older people use the same forms of communication to maintain relationships that Millennials do; they're just more likely to use some forms and less likely to use others. Millennials are more likely to communicate with others through social networking platforms, text, and instant messaging, while older people are more likely to use e-mail. In fact, the lament about people at work writing long e-mails to a colleague instead of getting up from their desk and walking down the hall to have the conversation is not a generation-specific issue. We have heard these complaints about how communication takes place in organizations since long before the oldest Millennials graduated from high school.

Like Millennials, a majority of workers from older generations say that they have friends at work[22] and can confide in people at work.[23] Only 28 percent say they are likely to socialize with people at work weekly or a couple of times a month, which means they are less likely to socialize frequently with coworkers than are Millennials. Like Millennials, older workers prefer receiving performance evaluation feedback, discussing career plans, and discussing compensation face-to-face when given the choice.[24] Three-quarters say that their teams have a great deal of personal meaning to them, they prefer working with a group to working alone, and they volunteer to do things to help their teams.

Overall, like their Millennial peers, older workers strongly value the social aspects of their job. Having friends at work is just as important for older workers as it is for Millennials and is a key determinant of how committed they are to the organization.

Millennials also want the people they work with to be their friends. Though you may have neither the time for nor the interest in hanging out, show an interest in their lives outside of work and tell them about yours. What interests do you have in common?

Just as you can coach and mentor Millennials at work, Millennials who are quite familiar with new technologies can reciprocate by showing you and your colleagues ways to make the best use of newer, unfamiliar technologies. For example, as the world moves toward figuring out how to conduct business over social media, it would be beneficial for you to expand your knowledge of these tools. Setting up internal social networking sites is a growing trend, and the benefits of collaborating with your coworkers can be substantial if done right. Millennials can help you learn how to do it quickly.

Recommendations for Managing Millennials

1. Let them use their preferred technology to support their work, if possible.

Every new generation is more adept at the current technology than its elders, and Millennials are no exception. As an organization, you know you shouldn't jump on the new technology bandwagon just because the young people are using something different and cool. But you also know that often there are real benefits to the new technology, including potential cost and time savings, that will benefit the organization. You also have to consider the risk of being left behind as society, your customers, and key employees shift to new processes. Giving employees the option to use the new technologies in appropriate ways can provide an effective path for introducing options to the organization.

As a manager, work closely with employees to understand the potential and drawbacks of new technologies. The most immediate short-term benefit may be just that employees are happier because they get to use the technology they prefer. But the time and effort invested to learn and understand why they are using it and what the new technology has to offer can yield a big return: accelerating your and your organization's ability to adapt to the new way that people are communicating and interacting with each other. The potential to protect or add to your competitive advantage means it's an investment you can't afford not to make.

2. Make sure you connect with your Millennial staff as people.

Employees don't want to be treated as just a number or a cog in the machine. Connect with them. Find out what makes them tick. Show that you actually care for them as human beings. This doesn't mean you have to cater to their every wish or go out with them every day after work, but the more you connect with them as people, the easier it will be to say no in a compassionate way when you have to.

As a manager, remember that even in the midst of all the pressures you and your team are under at work, taking the extra time to reach out to employees personally can yield huge benefits. We often feel like we don't have time for everything we have to do in life, and taking time away from whatever task we're thinking about to focus on the personal side of work can feel like a distraction. It will feel more important if you recognize the benefit your team members will get from being acknowledged for their whole selves, not just what they contribute on the job. Feeling connected may even help you in the long run.

3. In person is still almost always the best choice when communicating with Millennials, especially for anything related to compensation, development, or performance.

No one wants to have tough conversations over e-mail or text, and Millennials are no exception. Though they are comfortable with technology, they recognize the importance of nonverbal communication and strongly prefer that important conversations occur face-to-face. Even though employees may spend much of their personal time, and even some professional time, on social networks and instant messaging, those communication tools should not be used for critical conversations at work.

As a manager, remember that when discussing compensation, professional development, and performance reviews, there is no substitute for being there in person. Make every effort to have these conversations face-to-face. When managing employees at a distance where there might not be the option to have these conversations in person, ask them how they'd prefer to handle it. Some may prefer the phone, others video conferencing. The point is to be aware of their preferences and to make sure they receive the information in the way they prefer.

4. Provide opportunities for Millennials to make friends at work.

Organizations do not exist to create a social life for employees, but that does not change the fact that many, Millennials included, make friends at work. Employees like creating a community where they work, and friendships are a key part of that. The more opportunities you can provide to enable those relationships to develop, the better.

Managers and organizations can't provide people with friends, but they can create opportunities for people to meet and get to know each other in nonwork environments. For example, sports teams are common in many organizations. We heard of organization-based teams in France, South Africa, India, the United States, the United Kingdom, Canada, and Brazil, and we expect they exist in most countries; they just weren't mentioned. Some organizations find hobby groups a good way to help employees connect. For example, Starbucks has a Dragonboat group, Eli Lily a Chinese culture group, and Qualcomm sponsors team events such as pumpkin carving at Halloween. Through these sorts of groups, employees have opportunities to meet and make friends with people who have similar interests.

5. Be—or provide—good managers, and make coaching relevant to their job.

Work on improving your relationships with your employees because a healthy supervisor-employee relationship is as critical to Millennials as it is to everyone else. Managers can do this by being mentors as much as they are bosses. Most people respond to constructive feedback and positive coaching. Employees want coaching that they see as directly relevant to their current jobs and their long-term careers. They want to know how to be successful, and targeted coaching meets that need better than anything else.

Therefore, focus on how to improve their leadership and managerial skills. No one is perfect—we all have room for improvement. And no one notices your imperfections more than the people you lead, the ones who may spend as much or more time with you on a daily basis as does your own family (during the workweek—hopefully not also on weekends). Even though you undoubtedly have grown and improved as a manager and leader, people see the discrepancies today rather than the improvements from six years ago. So, hard as it may be, the best way to be a good manager to your team is to be constantly on the lookout for ways to improve.[25]

Five Points to Remember

1. Millennials' technology knowledge can help keep the organization current.
2. Millennials crave connection and community at work—with their friends and the teams they work with.
3. You can't replace face-to-face communication, even for Millennials.
4. Millennials need a good boss just as much as the next person.
5. Millennials want to be guided to success on the job and in their careers.

Who Millennials Are and What They Want

Millennials:
- Love technology and want all the tech toys they can get
- Believe technology reduces drudgery and saves time
- Prefer face-to-face interactions for critical communications
- Feel connections with friends are critical to their experience at work
- Maintain friendships through cyberspace
- Want a connection with their team
- Want a boss they like and trust
- Want to feel connected with the organization as a whole

CHAPTER 5

COMMITTED *AND* LEAVING

David has worked for his organization for eight years, three years man-aging the same group. He is considered a high potential, is regarded as the likely successor to his boss, and periodically is asked to update top executives on his initiatives (something that is uncommon for some-one at his level in this organization). He works long hours to produce excellent results for the company, and he is perceived by all as a highly committed and valuable employee. If you asked people who work with him, they would say David is exactly the kind of person they want and they only hope they can find more people like him to work there.

What they don't realize is that David isn't happy. While his pay is acceptable, it isn't good. He has had some opportunities to grow at the company and has been told there will be more, but they are slow in coming. He is given too much work and doesn't complain about it because everyone on the team is overworked. But it annoys him because he feels as if the company is taking advantage of him by not having enough staff to do the work. His boss is great—a real champion for him—but his boss can't eliminate the politics David sees permeat-ing the organization. So despite his stellar reviews and boss's support, he is looking for opportunities in other organizations—constantly.

When last we spoke, David was continuing to keep an eye out for good opportunities while still working hard at his current job. It isn't that he wants to leave. In fact, he wants to stay because he believes in the organization, likes his boss, and has had real opportunities to develop and grow both personally and professionally. But many days he wakes up in the morning feeling like he's being stifled in his cur-rent job. So he keeps looking, all the while being highly productive, and waiting for things to get better, so he won't have to leave.

MILLENNIALS ARE COMMITTED?

Millennials have been derided for a lack of commitment to their organizations. If we took the pessimists seriously, it would be easy to conclude that Millennials are ready to walk out the door at the drop of a hat. Yet our interviews and the data revealed a much more complex picture of the push and pull factors at play between Millennials and the organizations that employ them.

David is a perfect example. He is definitely committed to the organization. Yet he's keeping an eye out for other opportunities because he isn't completely happy with his current situation. He believes that if he keeps looking he is likely to find a position with better compensation, more opportunities, great people, and interesting work.

Millennials Are Committed . . . Because They Are (Mostly) Getting What They Need

Millennials are quite committed to their organizations. More than half[1] say they are emotionally attached to the organization, about two-thirds[2] say they enjoy discussing their organization with people outside it, and about two-thirds[3] don't intend to leave.

Why are Millennials committed? There are a variety of reasons, most of which are common to all generations. Among the most important are the following:

- They generally like the work they are doing. Sixty-nine percent say they are satisfied with their job.
- They like their organization. About three-quarters[4] say they like working for their current organization.
- They think their organization does work that has a positive influence on the world. Almost three-quarters[5] say that their organization behaves as a good corporate citizen.
- They feel that they have access to learning and development resources at work that will help them to improve their skills.[6]

- They believe that their organization values employee learning and development.[7]
- They have friends at work, and 98 percent say it's important to them to cultivate friendships at work.[8]
- The majority believe that their supervisors care about their well-being.[9]

Taken together, this paints a picture of Millennials who are generally committed.

The Point

Millennials are committed to their organization when they do work they enjoy, have access to learning and development, like their bosses, believe their organizations are having a positive effect on the world, and have coworkers they like and friends at work. Organizations that provide these conditions will reap the benefits that come from having a more committed workforce.

In Case You're Wondering about Older Employees' Commitment

Older employees:

- Generally like the work they are doing. Seventy-four percent say they are satisfied with their job.
- Like the organization they are currently working for (85 percent).
- Think their organization does work that has a positive influence in the world. Eighty percent say their organization behaves as a good corporate citizen.
- Say that they have access to learning and development resources at work that will help them to improve their skills (78 percent).
- Believe that their organization values employee learning and development (78 percent).

- Have friends at work, which 97 percent say is important to them.[10]
- Believe that their supervisors care about their well-being (58 percent).

○———————————————————○

Millennials Are Committed . . . They Don't Want to Leave

Contrary to the stereotype, Millennials don't prefer changing organizations every few years. In fact, Millennials would like to stay for a long time: about half[11] say they would be happy to spend *the rest of their careers with their current organizations.* In our interviews with Millennials, a majority said they really wanted to stay with their current organizations—for the rest of their working lives, if they could. They clearly like the idea of a long, stable career.

For example, one Millennial started with his organization at the age of 19 during a work-study program. When we spoke with him, he said that if he had the chance, he'd spend his whole career there (he was the ripe old age of 23 at the time). When we asked why, he listed the reasons described in the first section of this chapter: he liked his boss and the people he worked with, he had good friends at work whom he had fun with (even while working), the organization continuously provided him with opportunities to learn and grow, he was paid well enough, and he thought the organization did good work. He told us that he'd be happy to spend the next 40 years with the same organization. He wasn't sure it would happen, but he said he would be quite content if it worked out that way.

Many Millennials across the globe are planning to work for just one organization for a long period of time (see Figure 5.1). With the exception of Singapore, at least 40 percent of Millennials see themselves with very long tenure with at least one organization. The number is above 60 percent in Canada, the Netherlands, Mexico, Spain, the United Kingdom, Brazil, Germany, and the United States. This is different from the popular stereotype of Millennials wanting to frequently change jobs. The bottom line is that

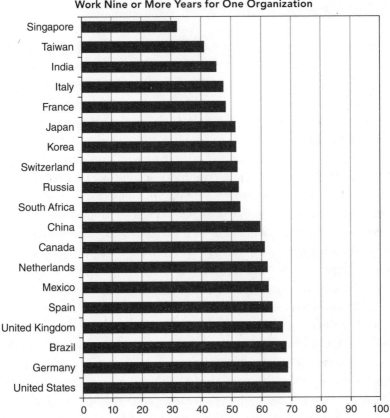

FIGURE 5.1: Percentage of Millennials Who Expect to Work Nine or More Years for One Organization

many people, Millennials included, do not like change for the sake of change, and changing jobs can be very disruptive. Unless they have a compelling reason to leave, people usually like to stay where they are.

The Point

Millennials would prefer to stay with one organization for most or all of their working lives if they could. A large percentage of Millennials around the world expect to be able to stay with their current organizations for a long time. Organizations that provide the conditions employees want will benefit from retaining the best staff.

Millennials Are Committed . . . They Want to Move Up Within an Organization

One common complaint about Millennials is that they aren't driven, that they don't want to move to the top and run organizations. Research doesn't support that conclusion. A Pew study done in 2013 showed that 70 percent of Millennial men and 61 percent of Millennial women would like to be a top manager someday.[12] Seventy percent of Millennials in Universum's global survey said that they wanted to rise to the level of manager or leader in their organizations.[13] Research by CareerBuilder reported in 2014 in *Harvard Business Review* indicates 52 percent of older Millennials (aged 25–34) aspire to a leadership position, in comparison with 67 percent of younger Millennials (aged 18–24). Both those numbers are higher than those for older employees (37 percent for ages 35–44, 23 percent for 45–54, and 20 percent for 55 or older).[14] The bottom line: a majority of Millennials want to become leaders in their organizations.

This is precisely what we heard from Millennials during interviews and focus groups. Millennials expressed their desire to move up within their organizations and to make a difference (and make more money). At the same time, they were concerned about the toll higher-level jobs would take on them and their (future) families because they saw the kind of lives their supervisors were living.

Millennials' supervisors had a similar perspective. They talked about how hard Millennials work, how many hours they put in, and how available they make themselves to ensure the work gets done. At the same time, they identified potential issues, such as Millennials still learning how to prioritize work and their personal lives. They saw Millennials' drive to move up within the organization but thought that many had not yet developed the necessary skills to advance.

Consistent with what was reported by Pew and CareerBuilder, what we see is more nuanced than "Millennials don't want to work hard enough to move to the top of the organization" or "Millennials don't want to get to the top of the organization because they don't want to work hard." We find that Millennials overall are just as likely as their older colleagues to say that they want to move to the top of their organization. In fact, Table 5.1 shows that at each level in the organizational hierarchy, Millennials are more likely than their non-Millennial (older) peers to say they want to move up in their organization and work in senior leadership positions.

We think there are three reasons for this difference. First, some Millennials haven't yet been exposed to the kinds of career experiences and setbacks that can lead people to temper their expectations and become satisfied with fewer promotions in their careers. Second, some Millennials are on faster career trajectories than their older colleagues—they have gotten to a comparable career stage in fewer years and therefore expect to continue to advance higher and faster than their older peers. Third, some older staff have a much clearer understanding of the pressures of working in higher-level roles and know they don't want to make the necessary sacrifices to their quality of life; similarly, some Millennials likely will adjust down their desire for promotion over time.

TABLE 5.1 Percentage Who Want to Get to the Top of an Organization

CURRENT LEVEL	MILLENNIALS	OLDER STAFF
Level 1 – Administrative/nonprofessional	13%	3%
Level 2 – Professional	26%	18%
Level 3 – First-level manager	23%	20%
Level 4 – Mid-level manager	31%	22%
Level 5 – Director/Executive	56%	44%

The Point

Millennials do want to move up within their organizations. They are career oriented and want to progress to higher levels of authority and power. Just as in any generation, there is variation among them—not every Millennial wants to be a captain of industry. But a large percentage of them do, and that percentage increases the higher their current position in the organization. Millennials certainly are not lacking in ambition to get ahead. Employees need clarity from their organizations on what they have to accomplish, learn, and demonstrate to be promoted.

COMMITTED DOES NOT MEAN STAY NO MATTER WHAT

Millennials may be committed to their organizations, but about a third[15] say they are looking for other opportunities.

This means that at least a third of Millennials are assessing the environment for better options *right now*—and even more will be doing so in the near future.[16] Some Millennials are trying to escape a situation they don't like, while others are trying to "level up" to a better situation, even if they are generally satisfied with their current situation. ("Level up" is a computer gaming term for moving to a higher level so you have access to better options in the game.) In other words, some are pushed to get out of a bad situation, while others feel the pull of wanting something better than what they currently have, even though they might be generally content to stay where they are.

Millennials are Leaving . . . Why They Try to Escape Their Current Positions

Sometimes Millennials leave to escape from unpleasant situations. Here are several examples of what they are trying to escape.

Overload

While Millennials are willing to work hard, at some point enough is enough. Many Millennials want to move from their current organization because they feel overloaded in their job, and they don't believe it will be better in another position in the same organization. Part of that is about a desire for work-life balance, and part is about just having too much to do and not enough time to do it. Feeling overloaded is common among Millennials: 42 percent believe they can't get everything done on their job, and 49 percent believe that because of the workload, they cannot possibly do all their work well.

The perception of being overloaded is an especially big problem for Millennials because of their orientation toward work. Remember, Millennials are highly intrinsically motivated, which means that they really care about the work they're doing. As a consequence, thinking they can't do something they care about well because they are overloaded is a big negative for them. They're likely to find that situation depressing and may want another job where they can do what they consider to be good work. Employees don't like to be trapped in situations where they feel they are doomed to failure from the start, which is what often happens to overworked employees. So rather than feel trapped, they find another organization where they believe the expectations are more reasonable.

You Can't Ignore Their Stress Just Because They Chose the Job

People who take on high-powered jobs obviously know they are going to have more responsibility and greater workloads than in lower-level, lower-pressure roles. So why should a senior manager or executive worry about complaints of work-life balance or career advancement for people who have chosen the high-powered job? Because how they feel about their job matters.

If they consistently feel they can't balance their work and their lives in a way they find acceptable, that can make them unhappy with their careers, result in poor performance, and compel them to leave for greener pastures. So whether or not you believe that people who choose high-pressure jobs should complain about work-life balance and career advancement, you need to understand that their feelings affect their commitment.

Millennials believe that if they control their work, they can reduce the overload. Sixty-six percent of Millennials say that having control over their work assignments is very or extremely important to them. (This is true for both men and women.) Slightly less than half[17] of Millennials believe that they can control their work pace.

We spoke with one Millennial who had a particular problem with this. She was a high potential and also a candidate for burning out. She routinely worked 12-hour days, and she hadn't had more than a day off in six months. She had to cancel her previous year's vacation—after it had been paid for—because her bosses told her she couldn't leave because it was a critical time for the business. She was a dedicated employee and canceled her vacation (the organization reimbursed her for its cost), but she didn't get to reschedule it *for another year.* She was a prime example of someone who was seriously overloaded with work.

While this woman's story is an extreme example, many Millennials experience work overload, some of which is unnecessary. Millennials are quite aware of how much more they could get done with more efficient technology and work processes. If they feel overloaded and see a fix that their organizations refuse to implement, they are likely to become even more resentful of the overload. If the overload could be reduced and the people in charge don't take the obvious steps to do so, that sends a pretty clear message to the Millennial: management doesn't care about the overload, so the Millennial should find a different place to work where it's less of an issue.

"If you work 24 hours a day, you won't need your apartment and that will save you a lot of money and that's the same as getting a raise!"

© Randy Glasbergen, glasbergen.com

Organizational Politics

Even when Millennials are committed to the organization and its mission and are well paid, organizational politics is one aspect of work that could cause them to leave. For example, Millennials are very likely to say that they are looking to leave their organization if they believe (1) that there is a politically powerful group within their organization that no one ever crosses; (2) that it is easier to remain quiet than to fight the system; or (3) that pay and promotion are primarily based on organizational politics. Millennials dislike organizational politics (as do their older colleagues), and the more they see it, the more likely they are to say they are looking for a new job.

Unfortunately, organizational politics is an issue many Millennials encounter in their organizations. We find that more than a quarter of Millennials believe organizational politics is a real, significant, and negative issue for their organizations. They believe that employees are more likely to get ahead if they keep quiet, agree with the people in power, and tell those people what they want to hear (for more details, see Appendix 5.1).

Organizational politics is an especially big issue for Millennials who have very sensitive hypocrisy detectors and who value honesty. We know Millennials have a desire to "speak truth." Millennials who work in organizations they perceive as being highly political—or for managers they perceive this way, even if the organization is more open—are likely to want to leave even if the organization is otherwise a good place to work. If they feel they can't make a contribution or advance because of office politics, and if being political rather than being productive is required for promotion, they will want to leave even faster.

Bad Management

There is an old truism: people do not leave companies, they leave bad bosses. That is as true for Millennials as it has been for older generations. While the majority of Millennials (58 percent) believe that their managers care about their well-being, the bad news is that 42 percent think that their managers *don't*. About a quarter don't feel their supervisors are supportive, say that their managers don't appreciate it when they put in extra effort, don't believe their managers are forgiving of honest mistakes, and don't think their managers understand when they have to prioritize their lives over work.[18] One in five say that their managers show little concern for them. That means that between a quarter and a third of Millennials don't feel their managers are meeting their needs.

"We've found that our new employees flourish when we treat them like mushrooms...keep 'em in the dark and feed 'em lots of manure..."

Source: CartoonStock.com

In addition, many Millennials don't trust their bosses much. Only 38 percent of Millennials say they trust their boss a lot, while 54 percent have some reservations about how much they trust their boss. About a third of Millennials report that their bosses order people around just because they can. These Millennials are flight risks.

Unacceptable Compensation

A majority of Millennials think compensation is important and are dissatisfied with theirs (see Figure 5.2; note that the same is true of older staff). They think their pay and benefits are not fair recompense for the skills and effort they put into their work. Further, they believe they are underpaid in comparison with their peers within their own organization and in comparison with those at other organizations at the same job level.

Why do most Millennials believe they are not fairly compensated? Because they are comparing notes with others about

FIGURE 5.2: Compensation Importance and Satisfaction

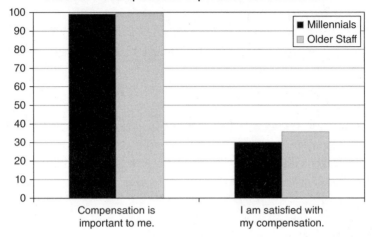

compensation, as we discussed in Chapter 3. It is likely that a majority of them have looked online to see what others are paid. While the accuracy of the data on these websites is often questioned, people still refer to them and are influenced by the information they find. In addition to looking at compensation comparisons online, a large percentage of Millennials discuss their compensation with their coworkers, family, and friends.

So *nearly all* Millennials think compensation is important, yet only about a *third* of them are satisfied with their compensation. Is it any wonder that many of them look for other opportunities?

The Point

Millennials will look to escape from situations where they have a bad supervisor, encounter too much office politics, feel overloaded, or think they are underpaid for the work they are doing. Organizations need to make sure that they are staffed to reduce overload, that managers are trained and have time to be good supervisors, that compensation is appropriate, and that the organization rewards productivity more than it does office politics.

Millennials Are Leaving... Why They Try to "Level Up" into a Better Situation

One of the best indicators that Millennials are committed is that the majority want to stay for a long time and are interested in becoming leaders in their current organizations.

But even those who are committed, feel generally happy with their situation, and say they would like to stay forever recognize that other opportunities might be a better fit for them. They could be perfectly content to stay in their current role, but they are drawn to "level up" to a new role that offers more compensation, better work-life balance, increased developmental opportunities, and so on. As a result, they keep an eye out for opportunities that would be an improvement over their current situation.

Better Compensation

Compensation is important to 99 percent of Millennials (see Figure 5.2) and very or extremely important to 81 percent of them. When they look to move to another organization, they are looking for greater compensation, either immediately or in the near future.

Millennials told us that they have real alternative job prospects that are potentially better than their current positions. When asked, more than two-thirds[19] said that if they wanted to move, they could find an acceptable position. Eighty-nine percent believe that they would be paid more than they are currently if they took a new job.

Around the globe, Millennials know (or believe they know) that they have viable options at other organizations. More than 50 percent of Millennials in most countries (see Figure 5.3) say that they know of other organizations that would offer them a job if they were looking. This makes the threat of them leaving both real and credible if they don't get the advancement, learning, and community they want from their current organizations.

Why do Millennials believe it would be so easy to find a job with better compensation? Part of the reason is undoubtedly because of how frequently many of them are called by headhunters about other jobs. More than 70 percent of Millennials said that they were

FIGURE 5.3: Percentage of Millennials Who Know of Organizations
That They Believe Would Offer Them a Job If They Were Looking

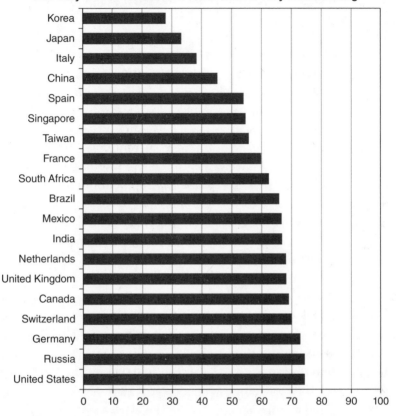

contacted at least once in the previous six months about a job at
another organization. For 30 percent it was more than four times.
And for 16 percent it was *10 or more times.*

These contacts aren't just calls. These conversations often
include discussions about salary ranges and promotions, as well as
learning and development opportunities at the new organization.
Millennials are often being pitched a new option that pays better
immediately and has better long-term prospects than their current
position. One way to think of these is as sales calls. The person calling has a job to sell to the Millennial, and the recruiter wants to
make the job as attractive as possible, while remaining relatively
accurate. So framing the job as having higher compensation and

greater development and advancement potential would benefit the recruiter. One manager questioned the reality being presented in these calls:

A Millennial who used to work for me received a call and was told about a new job where he would be paid 50 percent more, have a guaranteed promotion and pay increase in six months, be able to leave work earlier, get more professional development, etc. He went for the interview and was promised those same things by the company. After he received the job offer, he came back to me and asked if I could match it. I couldn't. I told him that I thought he was being sold something that wasn't going to happen, and I wished him luck. He took the job and left. I've heard from a few of his friends that the job didn't turn out to be everything he was told it was. I'm not surprised. In these cases, they rarely are.

Regardless of what people think is happening in these calls, whether they are presenting a realistic alternative option or a best-case scenario that almost never happens, they change the employees' reference points for their current positions. How much people think they should receive and how happy they are with what they receive are highly dependent on their reference points.

For example, Enrique found his compensation acceptable until he received a call from a headhunter. During the call the headhunter said Enrique could be making 30 percent more than he currently was if he took the same job in a different organization. He wasn't sure he believed her, so he asked around and found that both his peers at his current organization and people on websites that track compensation were being paid more than he was for basically the same work. A week later, he had a conversation with his boss about how unhappy he was with his compensation. Enrique's compensation hadn't been reduced that week, but his perception of it had changed as a result of the new reference points.

We found that this is a pattern globally. For example, India has a very hot labor market for highly skilled employees. Top talent among Millennials is headhunted frequently, and some move every 6 to 12 months for increasingly larger salaries. When we interviewed people in India, we asked about this and were told that it was common. We were also told that, not surprisingly, sometimes the new job turns out to be not all the Millennial was promised.

A headhunter selling these jobs as opportunities for advancement is capitalizing on a common worldview of Millennials. Millennials expect their compensation to go up, so people calling to offer them a position that pays more isn't a surprise. Millennials are as optimistic about their earning potential as Gen Xers were when they were younger.[21]

So *nearly all* Millennials think compensation is important, only about a *third* of them are satisfied with their compensation, and a *majority* of them get calls a couple of times a year suggesting they aren't making as much as they could be. Is it any wonder that many of them look for other opportunities?

Having a Life

Millennials will look for another position if they feel that their work-life balance is off. Almost two-thirds[22] feel work interferes with their personal lives. In many cases, these same Millennials work in organizations with work-life programs and initiatives. Unfortunately, about a third[23] believe that if they participate in work-life programs, they will be perceived as being less dedicated than those who do not use them. So they look for organizations where they believe they can meet their personal needs for work-life balance without being perceived as less dedicated for doing so.

For example, one man we interviewed talked about how important it was for him to play on his football (soccer) team. He had played on this same team for a few years without work interfering with his evening practices or his weekend games. But as he moved up within the organization, he found that work began to interfere. It wasn't just interfering with the occasional evening practice, it was affecting his ability to participate in tournaments on the weekends.

He was becoming increasingly frustrated because the demands were shifting from occasionally having to do a bit of work at home on the weekends or answering e-mails on his phone to being physically in the office on weekends. For the past few months, he had been required to come into the office for half-days almost every weekend, and as a result, he had missed some of his team's tournaments. He told us that if this pattern continued much longer, he would start looking for another job. While he said that playing a sport wasn't the most important thing in the world, it was important to him, and he didn't see why his work should consistently prevent him from having fun on weekends.

Part of the issue with work-life balance is the constant connectivity that is common for many employees today. In many organizations, Millennials expect to be connected with work almost all the time through their devices. Research shows that this is in fact their reality: many of them are in contact most waking hours of the day—and on weekends.

Given the constant connectivity, one aspect of their work that can help Millennials manage their need for work-life balance is the amount of flexibility the organization allows. Millennials expect flexibility. It is *critical* to them because of the way they live their lives, because they are independent, and because it is logical. While it makes sense that some work has to be done in an office at a particular time, it doesn't make sense to have no flexibility at other times.

Millennials are committed to their organization when it offers the work-life balance they want. When it doesn't, they look to leave because they believe they will get it somewhere else.

Better Development Opportunities

Millennials move to other organizations because they believe they will have more and better development opportunities there. Millennials are quite concerned about stagnation, both in their careers and in their development. Eighty percent believe that they need to continuously improve their professional skills and capabilities. They want to remain competitive in the workplace, they like to be challenged to do new things, and they feel strongly about making a contribution. They realize that if they don't continuously improve, they won't be able to grow and contribute to their organization.

Millennials place a high priority on development. Half say they work for a particular organization specifically because of the career opportunities. About three-quarters say they see their position as an opportunity to develop technical expertise,[24] develop leadership potential,[25] and demonstrate their abilities as a leader.[26]

Almost three-quarters say that they have access to learning and development resources at work that will help them improve their skills.[27] Yet about a quarter of Millennials tell us they are not getting the development they need to make them feel they are continuing to learn and improve.

One likely reason they don't think they're getting enough development is a lack of time. Though they have access to development, a majority[28] of Millennials say they don't have enough time to engage in development the way they need to. A number we spoke with said they weren't given adequate time to really think about and assimilate what they were learning (which is related to our earlier discussion about overload). They felt much of the learning was simply washing over them rather than being integrated into their work.

The lack of time for on-the-job development contributes to Millennials' perception that the organization is treating them as independent agents, not as valued contributors. From the Millennials' perspective, if the organization wants the employee to learn and is going to benefit directly from the employee's development, then the organization should provide the resources for the employee's development (e.g., both provide work time to do the development and pay for it). If the organization does not provide the resources, then the presumption is that the organization doesn't care that much about either the development or the employee. So Millennials move toward situations where they believe they will be more likely to get the development they need and have the resources provided to do it.

Better Promotion Opportunities

Millennials move to another organization because they believe they will have better opportunities for promotion at the new organization. Historically, many managers and leaders believed (and some still do) that people needed to spend a certain number of months or years in a particular position before they could really do the job well and gain all of the knowledge possible from that position.

The problem with that view is that people don't learn or integrate learning at the same rate. Think of it like learning geometry. Some intuitively grasp it and can work through the proofs quickly and accurately in a minimal amount of time. Having them do additional proofs for weeks on end will not result in a substantial improvement in performance. Other people don't intuitively get geometry. They really benefit from the additional time on task, and substantial growth can be seen over a much longer period of time.

The same is true at work, and Millennials realize this. They understand that they will master some skills quickly and others more slowly. What they don't accept is a manufacturing mindset that says that it will take a precise amount of time before they have learned everything they need to learn in that position. Millennials realize that everyone is different, and while a one-size-fits-all approach is efficient for an organization, it doesn't meet their needs as individuals. Remember, they believe organizations look at them as free agents, so they aren't going to trust organizations to keep them on staff for the long haul. They reject the idea of "wasting" a couple of years in a position beyond the point when they stop learning just to accommodate the organization's planning needs.

For example, a young woman in one organization had been in her position for a few years with consistently strong results. She was considered an excellent manager, and her work was highly valued by the organization. After a few years in the role, she felt she was stagnating. She asked to be promoted into a position in another division so she could grow and learn. She had found the open position on her own. The other division wanted her to fill the role but wouldn't take her without permission from her current bosses to move. She asked multiple times over nine months, and every time she asked she was told that it was an excellent idea and her bosses were working on it, but she did such a good job that it would be difficult to lose her. Even though they thought it would be difficult, they said they would figure it out. After nine months of this back-and-forth, she said that she wanted to be moved within six months. They agreed that would happen. And six months later she did indeed move—to another organization.

What happened? The organization didn't move her because it was inconvenient. The organization benefited from keeping her in her current position and would have been happy had she done the exact same thing for another 20 or more years. The organization looked at her as a cog rather than as a person who wanted to develop and grow—and who could leave if she didn't feel that she was developing and growing. They lost her because she wasn't willing to sacrifice her growth for the organization's convenience.

The belief that people should not have to stay in a role for a minimum number of years before being promoted is fairly consistent around the world. In most countries in our sample, a majority of Millennials (more than 60 percent) actively disagree with the perspective that people should expect to spend a minimum numbers of years in a job before they can be promoted (the exceptions are Korea, Taiwan, and China, where fewer than 40 percent of Millennials disagree; see Figure 5.4). In addition to those who disagree, 18 percent say they are neutral about whether people should have to stay in a position for a specific number of years. This means that, in all countries, at most one-third of Millennials say that people should stay in a position for a minimum number of years before they can be promoted, regardless of performance. That ranges from 7 percent in South Africa and the United Kingdom to 32 percent in China and Taiwan.

A key component of this perspective is the role of merit. Millennials who don't believe that people should have to stay in a position for a minimum number of years think that if people are qualified for promotion, if they are stagnating and not learning, there is no justification for holding them back just because someone believes they should be in the position longer. At its core, this is a generation, *globally*, that clearly believes in promotions based on merit more than on time in the position.

FIGURE 5.4: Percentage of Millennials Who Disagree That People Should Stay a Minimum Number of Years in a Job Before Promotion

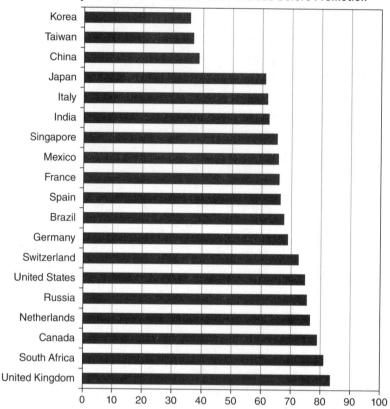

While the majority of Millennials in most countries are satisfied with their progress toward meeting their advancement goals (see Figure 5.5), the fact that more than one-third are dissatisfied with their progress indicates a large source of potential turnover.

For those who aren't happy with their speed of advancement, sometimes leaving is a good move for them because the organization really is too slow to promote, and the Millennial would stagnate if he or she stayed longer. On the other hand, sometimes moving up fast backfires, as shown by the story of a young man named Dave, who was a high flyer in his company. Dave's group had been responsible for revenues far above what was expected, largely because of his leadership. He agitated for promotion and

FIGURE 5.5: Percentage of Millennials Who Say They Are Satisfied with Their Progress Toward Meeting Their Goals for Advancement

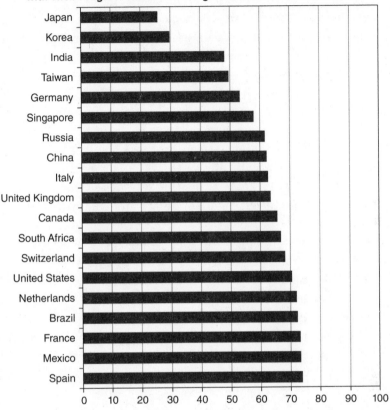

higher compensation and was promoted, received a pay increase, and was given a greater scope because of his team's performance. He was a big success story—until he crashed and burned. Though his team's performance was exceptional, his organizational maturity was not.

There were early inklings of his organizational immaturity—for example, when he was grandstanding about his contributions to the organization without giving credit to colleagues. When the boss saw Dave's pattern of behavior, he tried to get Dave coaching. He wanted Dave to understand the political nuances he was missing so he would stop burning bridges unnecessarily within the organization, but Dave refused. Dave believed that his performance would protect him. Besides, those other people were just trying to take credit away from him or get in the way of the great work he was doing because they were jealous. He continued to engage in behavior toward others that undermined his leadership and the leadership of his peers, including behavior that angered others for no productive reason.

Over time, the animosity grew, and eventually he was found to be doing things that were embarrassing to the company. When this came out, Dave was offered the choice of a demotion, so someone could help him develop greater organizational maturity, or leaving the organization. He left. This is an example of a situation where believing in promotion solely as a function of performance without the attendant organizational maturity resulted in derailment.

Both of these examples (the woman who eventually left after giving the organization plenty of warning and the man who left after a stunning display of organizational immaturity) are reality for some Millennials (and some older staff as well). Many employees believe they should be promoted solely based on performance and will start looking for other positions when they are not promoted despite their good performance. Others put in time and ask to be moved but aren't because the organization doesn't prioritize their promotion or development needs.

The reality in many cases is that employees may be ready for promotion, and you may want to promote them, but they can't move easily because a suitable position is not available—it's "blocked" by someone in it who isn't going to move any time soon. It is critical to find a way for these people to continue to learn and develop in their current roles through special assignments, additional responsibilities, and so on.

Many Millennials (and others) move to a different organization because they feel that their opportunities for development and promotion will be better at the new organization. Millennials are looking to leave, even while committed to the organization, because they want to keep learning, growing, and moving up. For Millennials, promotion is partly about building skills.

If they feel they are stagnating at their current organization, they will look elsewhere to make sure that stagnation does not continue.

Belonging to a Community at Work

When Millennials leave, they may be looking for an organization and coworkers whose values align with their own. If a Millennial decides that he (or she) doesn't believe in the mission of the organization or doesn't agree with the manager's priorities, he may feel he doesn't belong. This may cause him to look for a new job.

Relationships in the workplace also contribute to feelings of belonging. While Millennials may love technology, they also want to interact with people. Their relationships at work are critical both to their self-concept and to their commitment at work. But what happens if they work for a manager who doesn't prioritize getting to know fellow workers or developing close relationships with coworkers and, as a consequence, is dismissive of the Millennials? What happens if a Millennial isn't able to find friends in the workplace? That Millennial is more likely to feel out of place and will look elsewhere for a position that feels right.

For many Millennials, the feeling of belonging may be split between the organization they are currently employed by and the profession they have chosen. In many industries, one of the shifts has been away from employees feeling they are a member of the organizational family to feeling they belong to a profession and happen to work for one employer (for now). In fact, many Millennials personalize their professional membership in the way people in the past may have personalized their organization. For example, a majority of Millennials feel complimented personally when someone compliments someone else in their profession,[29] and they refer to other members of their profession (regardless of the organization they work for) as "we" rather than "they."[30]

This means that for many Millennials, "belonging" is partially independent of their organization. If they leave the organization, they take the sense of belonging that arises from their professional identification with them. So for some Millennials, the need to "belong" within the organization may be reduced by a strong feeling of belonging to their profession.

When Millennials don't feel they belong, they may start looking for what they are missing, whether that is an organization (or a manager) whose worldview is closer to theirs or coworkers and supervisors who care about them as people.

The Point

Millennials will look for a new job that raises some aspect of their life to a higher level. They often look to improve their compensation, work-life balance, promotion and development opportunities, or to find a sense of belonging to a community. Organizations that see retaining talent as a strategic advantage need to be aware of this desire to "level up" and provide options for employees that have this need.

CONCLUSION: MILLENNIALS LEAVE BECAUSE THEY BELIEVE THEY CAN GET SOMETHING BETTER ELSEWHERE

The evidence shows that while Millennials are committed, they may also be leaving. But people don't leave unless they have other opportunities they consider viable, and Millennials are no different. If the economy or something else prevents them from moving, they won't move. On the one hand, 37 percent of Millennials say that poor economic conditions have influenced their decision to stay in their current job in the past. On the other hand, currently a majority of Millennials say they could think of a number of organizations that would offer them a job if they were looking to move.

Millennials believe that jobs are abundant for them because headhunters often call many of them about other jobs and tell them they will have higher compensation and greater potential for development and advancement. In addition to better pay, a majority of Millennials believe that if they took an alternative job (with equivalent pay and responsibilities), they would work fewer hours. We might question whether this is a "grass is greener" phenomenon, where having more experience would provide the Millennials with a more accurate perspective of what is likely to happen. Evidence in favor of that interpretation comes from older employees' responses about the likely work hours in a new position: they were much less optimistic than were Millennials that their work hours would decrease (see Table 5.2).

TABLE 5.2 How Many Hours Would You Work If You Took a New Job?

TOTAL HOURS	MILLENNIALS	OLDER STAFF
Significantly more	2%	2%
Slightly more	8%	10%
Same hours	34%	50%
Slightly fewer hours	33%	26%
Significantly fewer hours	23%	12%

With their greater breadth of experience, older staff have a different perspective on alternative job opportunities: they don't necessarily believe it is going to be better somewhere else. Millennials, in contrast, are more likely to believe it is going to be better somewhere else, and they want that. They want to be where they have the best combination of compensation, interesting work, people they like, and work-life balance. Because they believe that there is something better out there, they keep looking for it.

Given that Millennials are simultaneously committed and leaving, the following sections describe some actions you can take to work more effectively with them whether you are a team member, a manager, or a leader.

Recommendations for Working with Millennials as Team Members

Millennials are very committed to the work, their teams, and the organization—for as long as they are there. While they may leave for a better opportunity, that doesn't mean that they aren't committed while they are working with their teams. They're willing to put in long hours and do what is necessary to get the work done.

How Different Are Millennials, Really?

Like Millennials, older employees are committed. In fact, a majority[31] would like to spend the rest of their careers with their current organizations.

Though they are committed, like Millennials, they are keeping an eye out for other opportunities. Similar to Millennials, they feel overloaded, don't feel they can control their work, aren't satisfied with their compensation, and feel that work interferes with their personal lives. A majority of those in the older generation believe they can't get everything done on their job,[32] and more than a quarter[33] believe that because of their workload, they cannot possibly do their work well. As with Millennials, it is likely that this is partly a result of not having control over their work. Having control over their work assignments is very or extremely important to them, but only about half believe that they can control their work pace, which is about the same percentage as Millennials.

Like Millennials, older staff think compensation is important, and most aren't satisfied (see Figure 5.2). Almost all (99.5 percent) of those older than Millennials say that compensation is important to them, but only 36 percent say that they are satisfied with their compensation. Similarly, about three-quarters of older employees have received at least one call from headhunters in the past year. Like Millennials, more than half34 feel work interferes with their personal lives.

At the same time, they believe that they have a responsibility to themselves to keep an eye out for better opportunities. They don't think the organization is going to look after their best interests, so they have to. This benefits those working with them—Millennials believe that they have to learn and perform well continually so they have greater opportunities for development and promotion. This attitude can help their coworkers continue to learn as well and achieve more.

Your Millennial colleagues can benefit from your experience. They value the advice and mentorship provided by their teammates, so if you have insights that would help them gain a more realistic understanding of their opportunities, share them. They will welcome hearing what you have to say about chances for promotion internally and opportunities at other organizations. At the same time, though, make sure you listen carefully to their hopes and desired career outcomes. No two people want exactly the same things from work, and it's important to keep in mind what Millennials want when you offer your perspective. Recall that they want guidance but don't want to be told what to do, so sharing your experiences needs to be just that. Share, but don't sound like you know what's best for them just because you were their age once.

Recommendations for Managing Millennials

People generally don't like leaving where they work unless things are going poorly. Even when they have really attractive offers elsewhere, it can be hard to leave everything and everyone they have worked with over the years. Millennials want to stay and contribute—if they are given the opportunity to do interesting work, to grow, and to be a welcome member of the team. Millennials value the friendships and community they build at work. They will often welcome the opportunity to stay so they don't have to give up the life they have built at the organization, but they will need your help to solve the challenges they are facing. Managers who work to make that happen will make it easier for Millennials to decide to stay.

1. Provide good management and minimize organizational politics.

If you want to retain employees and keep them happy, do everything possible to improve the quality of management and leadership.

This includes minimizing organizational politics. Employees are turned off when they see the role models above them engaging in counterproductive behaviors and being bad leaders.

People often remember the negative and don't remember the positive. One bad incident can have a much bigger impact than a collection of positive experiences. You can focus a great deal on making the organization a better place to work and getting rid of internal politics only to have your efforts undermined when a highly visible person does something out of line in a very public way. You and your peers on the leadership team may work quietly to reprimand that person because doing something quietly is often the best way to get such a person to listen, not be defensive, and fix the problem. Yet that approach is often invisible to the people who saw the initial bad behavior, so they may conclude that the offender got away with it. Keep this in mind and look for ways to send a message to the larger organization about what behaviors are acceptable or not, and how people are going to be held accountable for unacceptable behavior, and reinforce these messages as often as you can.

2. Help them get development.

Learning and professional development are key to what almost all employees, including Millennials, want from work. Providing them with developmental opportunities is a no-brainer: they benefit from the skill development and can apply those skills in future tasks while they work for you. Development can be a double-edged sword if you build employees' skills but don't give them an opportunity to use them—they might choose to leave for an organization that will put their skills to good use. It is very difficult to find the right combination of skills and organizational fit for people hired from outside, so developing your current Millennial employees and finding ways for them to use their newly acquired skills can provide one of the best returns on investment available anywhere.

Focus on creating these developmental opportunities for your direct reports. HR has a role to play in career planning, but the real responsibility for ensuring your employees get the developmental experiences they need falls on your shoulders. You are the one best suited to identify opportunities for them to develop on the job.

It has long been known that the best development happens through work. Classroom and online training are supplementary to the most impactful learning, which happens on the job. Working with your employees to figure out together where they need to improve and how to do it is one of the most important tasks for any manager. If you do it right, there's a double benefit. The employee will grow and be positioned to take on new responsibilities, and you will have an employee who is more dedicated, willing, and able to contribute because you gave her the opportunity to develop.

3. Make Millennials want to stay by providing good reasons to stay such as promotion, development, good pay, community, and good bosses.

You can greatly increase employees' desire to stay with your organization by getting the fundamentals right. Pay them right, and give them the opportunity to be promoted. Provide them with opportunities to find and work with people they get along with, both peers and supervisors. Do all of that and employee retention will be high.

Most important, keep in mind that employees decide to stay because of the entire package the organization provides, not just one aspect of the job, and that you help create that package for them. Most want either an actual promotion or at least some recognition that they are advancing in their careers. The opportunities to learn, apply that learning on the job, and be recognized by their supervisor and peers are aspects of the job they desire. A team that has a positive culture, where the team is productive and enjoys working together, can be a powerful antidote to the grass-is-greener allure of other organizations. The precise mix of what works will vary from person to person. Engaging employees in conversations about what they want and how to improve their job and the organization also helps.

4. Reduce overload and work-life imbalance—they are real issues that will drive Millennials away.

Burnout is a big issue in organizations today. As a result of many organizations' nonstop efforts to improve productivity and reduce labor costs, workloads have increased for most employees. Because

Millennials are the lowest in the hierarchy and least able to say no, they are particularly vulnerable to overload from too much work.

As a manager, keep in mind two important facts about workload and stress. First, just because you worked hard to get to where you are, that doesn't mean others will necessarily embrace that choice the same way you did. For some people, a daunting amount of work is a turnoff that can lead an otherwise highly productive person to walk out the door. Which is worse: easing some of the workload or trying to replace someone who leaves? Not only may a suitable replacement be difficult to find, but if you lose the headcount in your budget you may not get to replace the person at all. There are real costs to turnover: the decreased productivity of your group working with less than a full team, the financial cost to find and train a replacement, and the potential cost of losing the headcount. Reducing the workload, spreading the work among more people, or extending deadlines may be more cost effective than dealing with high rates of turnover.

Second, the demands of the workplace have increased over time. Companies continue to find more and more ways to squeeze ever greater productivity out of the same number of people. Part of this is about working smarter, which no one would object to (and which Millennials embrace). But the reality is that the sheer amount of work and the interruptions of home life have increased over the years. At a certain point, the volume of work can get to be too much, even for your most productive people. These dedicated professionals will work really hard for you, often making sure they finish that one last big project that absolutely had to get done—before turning around and walking out the door. That's what frequently happens if you ignore their real and legitimate concerns about work-life imbalance. The more responsive you are about relieving the stress of work, the less likely it is that Millennials (and other employees) will leave.

5. Provide development opportunities to bind them more tightly to the organization and improve retention.

Professional development is not about pacifying employees; developing your people gives your organization a competitive advantage.

When people are given the opportunity to develop and improve their skills and professional standing, they contribute more to the organization and are more committed to it. That binds them ever more closely to you and can reduce turnover.

Managers play a central role when it comes to their people's development. Some employees aren't aware of the available developmental opportunities. Some will have a good idea but will need help with the specifics. Others may know the details quite well but not feel comfortable asking to participate. And still others may think they should be able to take advantage of an opportunity for development but don't have realistic expectations about what's involved or whether they are suitable candidates for it.

While development is critical to retaining employees, it can feel threatening to take some of your best talent and send them off to do other things. Will they have enough time to get their regular job duties done? If they go on special assignment, who will cover their work while they are gone? If they get exposure to other parts of the organization, will that make them want to leave your group for another? These are all legitimate concerns, but none is an excuse for denying employees the developmental opportunities they need—if those opportunities make sense for both the person and the organization.

Though you might want to, you can't keep your best Millennials with you forever. It is likely they will want to—and need to—go and learn someplace else because their current position won't provide enough opportunities for them for the next 30 years. Rather than keeping them tied to you, there are benefits to helping them grow and explore other opportunities. You will be helping to develop the talents of employees who can contribute to your organization's success long after they have outgrown the tasks they are doing for you. And they just might stay longer and be even more engaged precisely because you trusted them and gave them the opportunity to develop, whether in their current positions or elsewhere in the organization. Both those options are better than having them walk out the door in frustration simply because you tried to hold them back. Yes, they may leave you to do something else within the organization. But better that than they leave the organization altogether—to work for your competitors!

6. Understand that they may not be happy with their progress, and that doesn't necessarily mean there is anything wrong.

Almost all employees, regardless of generation, want to progress as quickly as possible. So it's perfectly reasonable that Millennials will express their strong desire to progress and be promoted as quickly as possible. (On the flip side, when they don't, people claim that they aren't ambitious.) Yet employees' desire for progression and your organization's ability to satisfy their hopes and dreams may be very different.

As a manager, you don't need to worry about this (much) because the vast majority of employees are realistic about what an organization can do for them, even though they might not admit it to you. Though they may ask for the corner office, in most cases they realize they are more likely to get a small bonus or a relevant developmental opportunity. There's nothing wrong with stating clearly what you can and cannot do for them vis-à-vis promotions and development. You need to be aware, however, that if you don't satisfy their needs, they could decide to go somewhere that will. You have to weigh the cost of providing quicker advancement or additional learning opportunities (to improve the chances of advancement) against the cost of finding replacements if employees decide not to wait around for that promotion.

Five Points to Remember

1. Millennials will leave if their needs for promotion, advancement, development, community, and appreciation aren't met.
2. Millennials want to work within a community that matters to them—they want those they work with to care about them as people.
3. Pile too much on Millennials' backs and they will break—just like the rest of your employees.

4. Learning and growing are important to Millennials because they know they have to keep developing their skills to remain employable.
5. Millennials can leave—but they don't necessarily want to.

Who Millennials Are and What They Want

Millennials:
- Are committed to their organizations
- Like their work
- Feel like they are learning
- Want development
- Have friends at work
- Like their bosses and their organizations
- Would like to have long-term careers with their organizations
- Will leave if they can find a position that better meets their needs
- Are more likely to leave if they
  - Feel overloaded
  - Encounter too much organizational politics
  - Don't think they have good bosses
  - Think they can get better compensation elsewhere
  - Believe they will have better work-life balance elsewhere
  - Believe they will have better development and promotion opportunities elsewhere
  - Don't feel part of a community at work

CHAPTER 6

WHAT MILLENNIALS WANT, AND HOW TO GIVE IT TO THEM . . . WITHOUT GOING BANKRUPT OR ANGERING OLDER EMPLOYEES

While the details of how Millennials live their lives are different everywhere—what language they speak, how spicy their food is, which side of the street they drive on, how likely they are to live with their parents—Millennials are remarkably similar around the world. They like their jobs and their organizations, and they largely want the same things: an interesting, high-paying, stable job and working with people they like, trust, and feel appreciated by, in organizations that are socially responsible and value them enough to provide flexibility and opportunities for growth and promotion.

The organizations we work with have three primary goals for their talent management strategies for Millennials: attraction, engagement, and retention. They want to bring in the right Millennials and keep them engaged and committed to the organization. The three dimensions that help you achieve these objectives (see Model 6.1) are

- The people (friends and mentors, team, and boss)
- The work (interesting, meaningful, and balanced)
- Opportunities (feedback and communication, development, and pay)

MODEL 6.1: Talent Management Strategy for Millennials

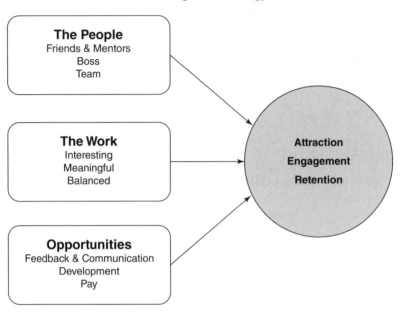

If you are particularly interested in attraction, engagement, or retention, you may be wondering if some of the dimensions are more important than others. The academic answer is "it depends," but the practical implications are simple: all of the dimensions are important for getting Millennials to work for you and be engaged and hardworking. The dimensions are mutually supportive and build on each other. We discuss each one in turn, followed by specific recommendations for actions you can take.

Commitment, Not Loyalty

Commitment is the foundation of healthy employment relationships. People talk about loyalty, but typically in terms of "Whatever happened to employee loyalty? Where did it go?"

Employee loyalty may have made sense in the past when the company man gave everything to the organization and received a long, stable (if not always rewarding) career in return. Yet that reality, if it ever really was the norm, ceased to exist in most places at least 30 years ago. Today, people believe they should be just as loyal to their organization as the organization is to them. And generally, they don't believe that organizations are loyal to their employees.

Therefore, it is more productive to talk about commitment, which is critical to employee productivity but doesn't imply that the employee will put the organization's needs ahead of his or her own.

The good news is that Millennials can demonstrate high degrees of commitment to the organizations that employ them. They can be strongly motivated to contribute and actually like the organization they are working for. They can be committed to do what it takes to help the organization succeed, if they are engaged the right way.

Organizations that provide the working conditions Millennials crave will benefit from a generation that is willing to work hard and stay long term. While Millennials may not be traditionally loyal, in the sense of staying with an organization no matter what, most Millennials would prefer to work for an organization for a long time. They will happily plan on spending a large part—or even all—of their career in one organization if the conditions are right. How do you make sure they keep working hard for you and not for someone else? For answers, read on.

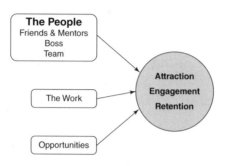

The People: Friends, Mentors, Team, and Boss

The community Millennials have at work is critical to their workplace experience. If they don't feel they have people they care about and who care about them, they are more likely to want to go elsewhere so they can develop those relationships. Most working professionals, managers, and executives spend more of their waking hours engaged with work (including commuting time) than they do at home during the week. That is also true for people in support roles, who usually work "only" eight hours a day. Millennials don't think their relationships at work are more important than their family relationships, but if they're going to spend so much time with the people they work with, they want those work relationships to matter. Organizations need to structure the workplace environment so Millennials can develop friendships with coworkers and have positive relationships with mentors, team members, and their boss.

Friends at Work

Friendships at work can be very important to Millennials. Among other benefits, having a good friend at work gives them an outlet for releasing stress when they need to blow off steam. It also indicates that they have a real connection to another person at work and, therefore, are likely to feel connected with the larger community within the organization. Millennials will respond well if your workplace provides opportunities for them to make friends at work and feel part of a community within their organization, beyond the people they work with on a daily basis.

Actions to Take

- **Create the conditions for friendships to flourish.** You can't force people to make friends with others at work; all you can do is provide a conducive environment. Think of it like trying to grow a plant: you can plant it and provide it with what you think it needs (soil pH, water, light, fertilizer, etc.), but it won't necessarily grow, and you don't always know why. All an organization can do is to provide opportunities for people to meet, get to know each other, and engage in activities together. For example, sports teams, interest groups, and clubs are ways people with similar interests can get to know each other and perhaps become friends. If you focus on creating an environment where people feel comfortable being themselves, where they are not penalized for socializing on the job (as long as they get the work done), then people will feel more relaxed and welcome at work. That in turn creates a foundation for the formation of friendships, if the right combinations of people encounter each other. It's that last crucial part that you can't control.

- **Support community building at work.** Help create a community at work, and involve the Millennials in the design and delivery of community-building activities. For example, one company we know of created councils with representatives from both the younger and older generations. The councils provided forums for airing issues and addressing both work-related and social topics such as how to resolve conflict on the job and where to go for advice on key topics. The councils also took responsibility for designing and delivering community-building activities at work such as social outings for employees and their families, celebrations of holidays and key events at work, and after-hours socializing.

Mentors

Millennials want mentors and generally like them when they have access to them. At their best, mentors are like extended family members who look out for Millennials, helping them avoid making mistakes on the job and with their careers. Millennials appreciate the special connections and insights mentors can provide and welcome their help as long as it's offered in a constructive manner.

Actions to Take

- **Set up formal mentoring programs.** Mentor relationships can be critical for Millennials, but not all of them will find mentors on their own. Formal mentoring programs may lack the spontaneity and informal nature that some mentoring relationships have, but having something is definitely better than having nothing. Give Millennials the option of trying different mentors until they find the right one.

- **Encourage people to take on mentees outside of formal programs.** In addition to formal programs, strongly encourage all of your leaders to take on mentees and to look for those not being advised by anyone.

- **Educate managers on promoting diversity and taking on mentees who are different from themselves.** People gravitate toward developing relationships, including mentoring relationships at work, with people similar to themselves. When there are demographic differences between the people with more experience in higher-level roles and Millennials in lower-level roles, those differences can lead to disparities in who has a mentor and who does not. For example, in organizations where men dominate management positions, women typically have more difficulty finding mentors. The same challenge exists for any ethnic or racial group not well represented in management ranks. For those at a mentoring disadvantage, formal mentor programs may provide the mentoring they need. But just as important is educating your managers on the importance of promoting diversity, including their role in reaching out and helping to develop those who are different from themselves.

The Team

The team Millennials work with is incredibly important to them. These are the people who form their most immediate community at work and with whom they spend the most time. They are the ones who, more than any others, can make or break Millennials' ability to get their jobs done right.

While for many organizations teams are the primary work unit and are responsible for most organizational performance, HR systems and performance management processes often reward the individual, not the team. This sends mixed messages to Millennials: the organization needs the team to perform well but focuses more on the employees as individuals than on the team.

The good news is that Millennials prefer working in teams. They want a connection with their team, will go out of their way to help team members, and expect everyone to pitch in when there are deadlines. Millennials are happy to take the approach of "we're all in this together," but they need their teammates, bosses, and the organization as a whole to do the same thing.

Actions to Take

- **Set the stage and get out of the way.** Many effective teams are self-led. This does not mean zero supervision from outside the team. But it does mean that the leaders the team members report to need to create the conditions for the team to succeed, step in to help realign it as necessary, and get out of the way so the team can solve problems and resolve conflicts on its own as much as possible. Millennials, who crave both independence and appropriate guidance, are well oriented to work under these conditions.

- **Improve team alignment.** One important factor contributing to effective teams is alignment among all the team members: Do they have a shared understanding of the team's objectives and how they are supposed to be accomplished? If this shared understanding is in place, then the team won't spend countless hours clarifying their goals and work processes. Common approaches to achieving alignment include gathering all team members together at the start of a project, or when new members are introduced, to make sure everyone knows each other and agrees on the team's objectives and plans to achieve them. Getting

everyone together face-to-face may be impractical for geographically dispersed teams, but members can still convene virtually
via conference calls, webinars, and videoconference sessions.

- **Improve team trust and support.** Trust among team members
  is a key benchmark of an effective team. You can't manufac-
  ture trust, but it absolutely is something to be nurtured. Do
  Millennials and their teammates feel like everyone else on the
  team can be trusted to do their work? Do they step in and help
  each other out to ensure deadlines are met? Team leaders and
  members need to be on the lookout for unproductive friction
  in group dynamics and work to help smooth it out early before
  it has a chance to fester and render the team dysfunctional.
  Depending on the issue, solutions can range from talking to
  a team member quietly on the side, sitting conflicting members down together to address the issue, or bringing the whole
  group together for problem solving. If trust and support behaviors are not in place, help the team figure out where things are
  not working well and devise ways to improve the situation.

- **Provide the resources the team needs to succeed.** An under-
  resourced team cannot function to the best of its abilities.
  Cost-cutting without an assessment of its negative impact on
  team performance can lead to lower costs in the short term but
  hurt much more down the line when teams can't deliver. Recall
  that Millennials don't automatically trust the organization and
  authority figures to do the right thing, and they want to belong
  to an organization that provides them with adequate resources.
  When Millennials see managers ensuring their teams get the
  resources they need, it sends an important signal that their
  work as team members is valued as well.

- **Hold everyone on the team both individually and jointly
  accountable for results.** Teams have to be held collectively
  accountable for their performance. Traditional performance
  management approaches tend to focus on individual contributions with little to no validation that those contributions

helped the team succeed. Team-based evaluation and rewards are needed to ensure a complementary focus on the ultimate outcomes that matter. Rewards can and should have both individual and team-based components. Even if only a relatively small amount of pay is based on the team's performance, the signal that the group's output matters for evaluation and rewards is critical in and of itself.

Bosses

Millennials' managers have the greatest power to impact Millennials' experiences at work. It is commonly said that people don't leave organizations, they leave their bosses. This is just as true for today's Millennials as it was for Gen Xers and Baby Boomers. And it is just as true in New York as it is in New Delhi.

Managers are the focal point for the overwhelming majority of experiences an employee has, so managers need to keep in mind the powerful impact they have on their direct reports. For example, consider a developmental opportunity that is supposed to be available to all employees, such as taking on a special assignment to work with customers. A manager might not want one of her direct reports to take the special assignment. Perhaps she is worried about him finishing his work for her team on time if he takes it on, or maybe she fears he will ask to transfer out of her group after having exposure to the other part of the business. Though she does not tell him her concerns, her direct report picks up what he believes to be discouraging signals from her and decides not to participate. He is worried about negative repercussions for his performance reviews and chances for promotion. All this happens even though she never says a negative word. She doesn't realize the signals she's sending and how her direct report is reacting to them (and he never tells her because he thinks she's sending the signals on purpose).

Millennials want to have good relationships with their managers. They look to their manager for approval and appreciation. They want to be guided to be successful on the job, and the manager is the primary person to guide them. The manager plays an important role in coaching Millennials, not just telling them what they have done wrong but also showing them how to improve. Showing that you trust them to do their job builds their confidence and commitment to you and the organization. Equally important is showing them that you are trustworthy and will follow through on what they need from you.

Actions to Take

- **Don't just talk—listen, observe, and make sure Millennials know they are appreciated.** Being a manager is a difficult job. Given how much managers have to do, it is often nearly impossible to do all parts of the job well. As a manager, one of the most critical things you can strive to do well is to be appreciative of the people who work for you. While managers have good intentions and typically make an effort to express their appreciation for good work, we find that employees need to be told they are appreciated even more often than they currently hear it.

- **Trust and be trustworthy.** Millennials want to trust and to feel comfortable relying on the people they work for. To earn that trust, their managers need to set them up for success and give them room to perform. Managers also need to demonstrate that they are trustworthy by doing what they say they are going to do, being honest, and helping out when they see that their assistance is needed. Providing the support Millennials' teams need to succeed also builds a strong foundation for Millennials to trust their managers.

- **Set goals and hold Millennials accountable.** Goal setting is a very important driver of performance for both Millennials and older generations. When you set ambitious but not overly aggressive goals, the motivation to meet the goals drives high performance. The danger lies in setting goals that are too aggressive, as they can seem unobtainable from the outset and might be demotivating. Giving everyone the same chance to succeed and holding employees accountable for performance sends a strong signal to Millennials that their efforts will be rewarded on par with those of their older colleagues.

- **Provide mentoring and support.** People grow faster if they have mentoring and support so they know what to do and have the opportunity to do it. Mentoring is especially important to Millennials in their early career stages because it can help them figure out what type of work they are best suited for.

- **Be authentic.** The authenticity of messaging sets an important tone for Millennials' trust of their manager. A manager who pretends something isn't true or tries to sweep sensitive or less-than-flattering information under the rug, will not be perceived as honest and trustworthy. Difficult as it may seem, if you can't be honest with everyone about a sensitive topic, the best response may be no response at all—it certainly beats lying if you want people to trust you.. Or you can acknowledge that there are some issues, the relevant details of which will be revealed at the appropriate time. Whatever approach you choose, the more authentic and honest the messaging, the better people will feel and the more Millennials will trust you.

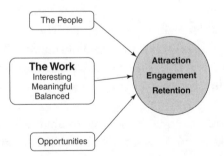

The Work: Interesting, Meaningful, and Balanced

For Millennials, both what they do and how they do it are critical to their workplace experience. Organizations that want to attract and retain Millennials will need to structure work so that it is interesting and meaningful and enables them to enjoy a balanced life (see Figure 6.2).

Interesting and Stimulating Work

Everyone dislikes boring work, and Millennials are no exception. They are strongly motivated to do good work, but it has to be work that is interesting. Of course, not all work is going to be interesting. But minimizing boring work offers the opportunity to engage Millennials to improve work processes. For example, engaging Millennials in brainstorming and decisions about the work design can push them to understand and accept that there may be no way around the repetitive, dull work that has to get done. As likely as that outcome is, they may also surprise you: they may find process improvements that make everyone's work more interesting and efficient.

Actions to Take

- **Give Millennials interesting work to do.** There is no real substitute for interesting work. If the work is interesting, it doesn't require a lot of convincing or clever framing by management to make it palatable. Therefore, the most effective approach is to give Millennials work that is actually interesting and will help them learn and grow and become even better contributors to the organization. But that isn't always possible, so . . .

- **Make sure Millennials are clear on the business reasons** for the tasks they are given that they find boring, and show how what they do contributes to the organization's objectives. This is particularly important for Millennials who have jobs where a large percentage of their time is spent doing routine and monotonous activities. For example, reviewing details for a client's contract can be tedious, but it is a critical task that is essential for the work to be successful. Also, showing appreciation for the boring and monotonous work employees do can lessen its negative impact on them.

- **Outsource it.** Outsourcing is an option to consider when Millennials complain about having too many routine and monotonous work tasks. Outsourcing is not a one-size-fits-all answer: some tasks cannot be shipped off site, and others you want to keep in house because they provide valuable learning opportunities for employees. If you can peel off a few of the more routine and monotonous tasks and outsource them to people who focus on that type of work, the more varied and interesting tasks can be done by your core employees.

- **Encourage Millennials to provide ideas to improve work processes.** People who have the opportunity to shape how their work is done take greater ownership and are more engaged with their work. Including Millennials in job design decisions can be threatening to leaders who like to hoard power, but that's precisely why frontline engagement in problem solving can be so powerful: it breaks down traditional lines of authority and sends a clear message of inclusion and respect to employees at all levels. The ideas can range from small, mundane changes to a large-scale redesign of the job.

  Examples of big changes include redesigning the end-to-end process of how work is done in the group, deciding which vendor to select for a large-scale technology implementation, or letting the group determine how performance awards are handed out among team members. Small changes could include setting the time for meetings according to team members' preferences rather than the leader's, deciding on a less formal dress code, or letting the group decide who gets to go to certain client meetings. Don't discount the benefits of small changes. While they may seem less meaningful to leaders, if they remove sources of boredom and frustration, the benefits in terms of increased engagement and job satisfaction can be quite high.

- **Provide opportunities for Millennials to interact with the outside world.** A key to keeping Millennials engaged is development, which means offering them new and different types of experiences at work. Provide opportunities for Millennials to engage with the outside world (customers and stakeholders) through assignments in other locations (including overseas, if possible), task forces that enable them to interact with the community, jobs that expose them to different segments of your customer base, and so on. These opportunities are valuable not only because they build employee skills in different ways but also because they help satisfy Millennials' desire to engage in interesting work.

Make the opportunities available to as many team members as possible, including planned rotations of people into the opportunities, instead of keeping the same people in place because they are doing a great job. The short-term transition costs of bringing in someone new will be worth the longer-term benefits of having more people engage in the work. The result will be a deeper bench of people who can step in to fill those roles in crunch situations, such as when someone leaves unexpectedly.

- **Leverage Millennials' desire to use the latest technology.** Your IT strategy should not be driven by the latest fads adopted by Millennials, but ignoring emerging technologies can pose big risks. Every new generation is more familiar with emerging technologies than the older generations, and Millennials are no different.

  Consider the recent history of smartphone adoption at work. In the early stages of smartphones, when the iPhone was really taking off, most corporate IT departments resisted allowing their employees to use their personal smartphones at work for fear of security breaches. Yet once the door was opened to linking iPhones with corporate networks, employees happily started offering up their personal devices so they could enhance their workplace productivity.

  Tablets provide another example of how a relatively new technology championed by Millennials is becoming increasingly pervasive as a business tool. Many companies are replacing old devices with tablets that have both greater business functionality and the "wow" factor that attracts and retains Millennials. Your Millennials will be happy to help you pilot and exploit the power of the Next Big Thing to enhance work processes and improve productivity.

Meaningful Work

Millennials are not a monolithic group—not all of them want to change the world, though some clearly do (as some part of every young generation does). Broadly speaking, they want to engage in doing work *they* feel is meaningful with organizations *they* believe are good corporate citizens. What precisely that means varies from one Millennial to another, but you can still implement strategies to meet their needs and create win-wins for both them and your organization.

Actions to Take

- **Connect the work the Millennials are doing to positive social outcomes.** Just as you try to connect Millennials' work to the organization's goals and mission, you can help Millennials understand how their work is connected to outcomes that benefit society in both big and small ways. For example, a tax preparer helps individuals manage their finances. A consultant can help people and work processes become more effective so employees can get home to their families more quickly. A company that provides high-quality consumer products at affordable prices helps families afford things that otherwise would be beyond their reach. An electric utility provides life-sustaining power that enables people to live their lives. And so on. Whatever the company's mission, the manager should be able to connect the work an individual is doing with a larger purpose, and the larger purpose should have a positive impact on society.

- **Offer company-sponsored volunteering.** Company-sponsored volunteering events are relatively easy to do, and they do not have to involve large outlays of cash or paid time off. For example, collecting clothing and bathroom products for homeless shelters can be organized in the office. If you create the opportunity for people to get involved in company-sponsored volunteering, they often will give freely of their own time outside of working hours to support it. Some of the activities should be conducted as time off provided by the organization to show the organization's sincerity in supporting the community, but not all activities have to be. The people leading the events should be those who have a passion for the cause and who want to get the organization involved primarily for the benefit of the people being served, not because of the PR value. There is nothing wrong with doing a little bit of PR; just don't do it so much that people think publicity is the primary reason the organization is involved.

- **Do a better job of explaining your organization's contributions relative to others in the same industry.** It may be difficult, but one thing your organization can do is to assess how your business contributes to improved community outcomes, whatever industry you are in. We recognize there are limits to how much your organization can contribute directly to society. The key is not to compare your organization to organizations in other industries whose whole business is structured to do good in one way or another (like emergency room doctors saving lives on a daily basis or firefighters rescuing people from burning buildings).

  However, you need to think about how you perform relative to realistic expectations for organizations in your industry, especially relative to your competitors. For example, some automotive companies take a more proactive approach to dealing with reducing energy use even if the ROI hasn't been established yet, whereas others continue with their historical strategies. We expect the former to be more appealing to Millennials who care about meaningful work. You also can make donations of goods and services to community-based organizations and thus show that you are a socially proactive organization with which Millennials can identify.

Work-Life Balance

Millennials want to have a life as well as to work. If you pile so much work on Millennials' backs that they feel they have no time to live their lives, they'll do their best to get out from under the weight—just like the rest of your employees.

Therefore, organizations and managers need to employ options that help promote work-life balance. To start, Millennials want as much control over their work as possible. Letting Millennials control their work could be a bad idea if "control" meant "get to do whatever they want." But even the most demanding Millennials (well, almost all of them) will admit privately that they really only expect reasonable accommodations.

What constitutes reasonable in this case may be a lot less than you would expect. Reasonable Millennials (almost all we have spoken with around the world) realize that they can't redesign the whole organization to suit their personal preferences. Yet they also don't want to be treated like mushrooms (kept in the dark and fed manure). Millennials want to understand the reason for the tasks they are given, make choices about when and where the work is done, and have the chance to influence or even directly make some decisions about the work design.

The sheer volume of work can drive Millennials away as well. Reducing the amount of work can feel like a much harder nut to crack, but it's just as important as flexibility, and sometimes more so. Figuring out how to reduce the overall workload, and not just spread it out over a longer workday for each individual, can yield much greater returns than flexibility. You may end up spending a little more on headcount and/or consultants and outsourcing services, but you will reap the returns from lower turnover, greater effectiveness, and better knowledge retention.

Actions to Take

- **Don't require face time for its own sake.** Millennials have a strong aversion to putting in face time at work simply because that's the way it's always been done. Making people wait around just in case the boss might need them isn't much better—it may be justified in theory but drives people crazy. If the team is working on a tight deadline and the boss needs people available to check a report in the evening, try to find options such as letting workers go home and come back, or have them agree to be available for a conference call or e-mail exchange in the evening from home.

- **Set up the system so working off site is productive.** Moving away from a face time culture to something else can be threatening to managers who are not used to working that way. The key to a successful solution is striking the right balance between work demands and employee preferences.

  Extensive research and decades of experience in organizations have established unequivocally the benefits of working in the same place at the same time. Yet research and practice have also shown that working from other locations, including from home, can be just as productive as working in the office—if the right conditions are in place. For example, concentrated individual work on a document or spreadsheet can often be performed just as efficiently away from the office as it can at the office if the necessary technology is available.

  The key lies in identifying which work can be done away from the office, making sure everyone understands the timeline and deliverables, and establishing working relationships that function effectively when two people are not working side by side. This can take time and effort to get right, but once it's done, the up-front investment can pay dividends many times greater for months and even years afterward. Managers need to be educated on the benefits of allowing their people to work away from the office and on ways to do it well. At the same time, Millennials need to be educated on the importance of building relationships through in-person interactions, being in the office when needed, and making sure they are available when they decide to work off site.

- **Allow for flexible careers.** Flexible careers can be another critical part of a successful Millennial work-life balance strategy. People go through stages in their lives. People who were able and willing to work long and hard hours at one point in their careers may shift into a period when fewer work demands and slower career progression are preferred.

The old way of looking at careers often came down to all or nothing: either you were on the fast career track or you weren't, and if you got off it, there was no getting back on. Up or out were the only options. Today more and more companies are realizing that isn't the most effective approach for keeping the talent they want to retain long term. They find that there are substantial benefits to providing employees the option of pressing the pause button on career advancement. The reason for the pause could be having a child, caring for a sick or elderly family member, or just wanting to slow down and smell the roses for a few years.

Whatever the individual motivation, providing flexible career options sends a powerful message to Millennials that you want them to think about working with your organization for a long time, through both thick and thin.

- **Smooth out spikes in the workload.** A lot of work ebbs and flows throughout the year in predictable patterns. Some seasonality is driven by consumer patterns such as holiday shopping sales and products that are better suited for warm versus cold weather. Other ebbs and flows are tied to key events such as annual meetings, quarterly financial reporting, and so on. Organizations often fall into a pattern of not anticipating these shifts and having to do huge ramp-ups quickly.

  While it can feel heroic to put in a lot of effort, work really long days, and just manage to beat the deadline for the report, presentation, or delivery of products, this pattern takes its toll on the employees involved. If the group is led by an adrenaline junkie, the manager may look forward to those times, both for the bonds that are forged with coworkers and the thrill of beating seemingly unbeatable odds. Yet managers who work like this often create unnecessary work for their teams because they neglect to get the work started far enough in advance— and that's a real problem.

Whenever there are predictable spikes in the time and effort needed to meet key deadlines, a more proactive and prudent approach is to start as much of the work as possible ahead of time ("pulling the work forward" in the calendar). There are limits, of course, to how much work can be pulled forward. But doing so yields two very positive benefits: (1) a strong signal that you care about the team members' level of stress and are actively working to relieve it; and (2) a reduction in workload during the peak period (which will be appreciated). Even if it's just the difference between working, say, 50 versus 55 hours per week during crunch time, that small reduction in hours is felt by everyone and can make the difference for those who are most stressed and closest to walking out the door.

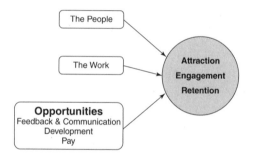

Opportunities: Feedback and Communication, Development, and Pay

For Millennials, feedback and communication, development, and pay are all critical to their workplace experience. If they don't get enough feedback, they don't know how they're doing, and they start to wonder if anyone is noticing their good work. If they don't get enough development, they start to worry that they are stagnating and won't be competitive in the job market (something they are always concerned about). If they don't get paid enough, they worry about bills and debts and the long-term consequences of their current pay level. Organizations that want to attract and retain Millennials need to make sure to provide them with enough feedback, development, and compensation for them to feel they are continuing to progress even as they stay with the same organization (see Figure 6.3).

Feedback and Communication

Millennials want to know what they need to do to be successful. At the same time, Millennials don't want to be micromanaged (who does?). So remember to approach them with guidance and coaching, not command-and-control dictates.

Millennials are very open to offering their opinions and are often willing to say what they think to people above them in the hierarchy. Rather than view this as a negative, embrace it for the benefits it can provide your organization. Having people who want to contribute is good; their actions just have to be channeled properly.

The good news is that Millennials want their opinions to be received in the right way. They believe there should be a clear chain of command. Even though they don't always trust authority, they are willing to follow it. But they need the appropriate outlets to make sure their voices and suggestions are heard. When you provide those, and show them you listen, that helps to build trust and ensure they will continue to speak up in appropriate ways. Appreciate their willingness to speak up, and encourage their desire to contribute.

Actions to Take

- **Coach and guide; don't tear down and order.** It should go without saying that Millennials (and people in general) handle constructive criticism much better than negative feedback. Yet managers often fall into patterns of being overly critical without providing useful advice on how to improve. Providing criticism that is constructive and the employee can act on is particularly important for Millennials who are sensitive to being micromanaged and told what to do in unconstructive ways. Typically, people don't deliberately do a task poorly. Often, they honestly don't see the difference between what you want and what they have done. While it is important to point out when work is deficient and things could be done better, make sure that you coach Millennials on how they can improve. Part of a manager's job is to help his or her employees learn to see the difference and perform at a higher level.

- **Provide feedback as a normal part of the workflow, not as an annual event.** Formal performance management processes ensure that feedback typically occurs at least once a year. But it shouldn't be *only* once a year—that is way too infrequent to help Millennials improve. Feedback of one form or another should happen at least every week or as frequently as work is delivered. Feedback that has an effect (rather than just being pro forma) should be based on the work itself and the person's need for information about how he or she is doing and how to improve. This is one of the most important activities a manager engages in, and yet it is typically not done often enough—especially for Millennials.

- **Everyone listens; everyone speaks.** Two-way communication is important. Sometimes people at the bottom feel that people at the top always talk and don't listen. Managers believe that if they say "my door is always open" or "you can come talk to me any time," they've done enough to encourage employees to be open with them. It isn't enough. Be specific about the communication. Follow up to understand how the message was heard and interpreted. It is critical for Millennials (and for everyone else) that people at all levels of the organization feel they have a chance to speak, and that both they and others also listen. From the top down, talking should include sharing strategy, vision, and key information in a timely fashion. For the top, listening means providing lower-level employees with opportunities to make suggestions and provide their perspective, as well as hearing and responding to what the frontline employees say.

- **Help Millennials learn how to speak their truth, constructively.** Closely related to the issue of two-way communication is helping

Millennials feel empowered to say what they think. If Millennials don't feel their voices are being heard, or if they feel that they are frequently being disregarded, they will find other ways to be heard such as publicly tweeting their thoughts or sharing them on social media sites. Such avenues for expression may end up being substantially more disruptive to the organization and harmful to Millennials' careers.

If you provide them with effective channels for contributing their input in a meaningful way, you can ensure productive communications that keep Millennials engaged and not stigmatized for challenging authority disrespectfully. For example, when thinking about how to improve their work, invite Millennials (and their older colleagues) to make suggestions about what could be improved—and then make sure you follow through on making the changes they recommend that are reasonable and add value. If you don't accept or implement their ideas, explain why or offer to discuss it with them.

However, make sure that you put forth for consideration only aspects of the work where the organization is ready and willing to make a change. Any aspects of the work that are viewed as immutable and not candidates for change should be excluded entirely from the process, and you should explain why they can't be included.

- **Have important career-related conversations with Millennials in person.** While using social networking sites is fine for socializing and even for some work-related communication, all important career-related communications with Millennials should be done in person. Given restrictions on travel budgets, it may be difficult for managers of Millennials who are working in other locations to have all important conversations face-to-face. Even when this is the case, managers should make every effort to have substantive conversations in person to develop the relationship as much as possible.

- **Help Millennials learn to have conversations others consider to be important in person.** While Millennials want conversations they consider important to *them* to be held in person, they don't always prioritize in the same way how they convey information *others* consider important. Managers need to help Millennials learn that they should use face-to-face communication for information others consider important, rather than whatever is most expedient for them. Given restrictions on travel budgets and the impracticality of meeting people in person who work far away, it's natural to default frequently to something other than face-to-face for many business communications. Millennials may need guidance in some situations to strike a good balance among electronic, telephone, and in-person communications, thinking about what best serves the needs of the receiver of the communication, not necessarily the preference of the Millennial.

Career Development

Millennials want to develop and move up within their organizations. Learning and growing are important to Millennials because they know they have to keep developing more skills to remain employable. But development is about much more than just keeping themselves gainfully employed or improving their chance of promotion. The learning that takes place makes the work more interesting, regardless of whether the learning is due to a carefully scripted development plan or just the normal exposure to new experiences on the job. And more interesting work makes the job more attractive to Millennials.

Provide Millennials with good development opportunities, or be prepared for them to go elsewhere to find them. Encourage their learning, development, and desire to rise within the organization. Help them develop, because everyone benefits when Millennials get development—Millennials, their managers, and the organization.

Actions to Take

- **Help Millennials realize that they'll learn the most on the job.** Once people start working, most development happens on the job, not by sitting in a classroom, watching a video, or taking an online training course. People who are recently out of school (as many Millennials are) may still believe that they need to be in a class to learn and that they need to demonstrate performance on a test so people will know that they've learned. Help Millennials understand that what they learn is for *them* to improve *their* careers, and that most of the time the only test they'll have is how they perform every day, day in and day out. Therefore, they are responsible for figuring out what they need to learn and whether they've learned enough. All everyone else sees is performance.

- **Have a plan for developing Millennials on the job.** Helping Millennials to establish appropriate career expectations through formal development planning is the first step. Following through on those plans is the second, which requires coordination among the Millennial, the boss, and the organization.

  As a manager, you may want your people to take charge of their own careers, but not all of the people reporting to you know what opportunities are available. Equally important, not all of them may be able to choose the opportunities that will have the greatest benefit for them and the organization; they may need your help to understand if they are a good match for a particular opportunity.

  Don't mistake being quiet for lack of interest or desire to be developed. Some people are less assertive about speaking up for themselves. Make sure they get the necessary attention, not just their more outspoken colleagues. Take the lead, and engage Millennials in conversations about development options and career directions.

- **Don't ignore the B players.** A professional friend of ours once remarked that organizations spend so much time focusing on the A players that sometimes they ignore the Bs. This spot-on observation highlights a fact that needs to be corrected: most organizations spend too much time and energy worrying about their stars and don't spend enough time on the ones who haven't yet emerged as stars—or who never will.

For all the value that the A players provide, they are a relatively small number. The much larger group of good performers is responsible for the vast majority of the work and deliverables that keep your organization running and your customers happy. Frequently the B players do not receive enough attention, leaving many of them frustrated with their lack of access to plum assignments and fast-track career paths. Millennials are earlier in their careers, and therefore you may find a lot of them in the B player group. Anything you can do to pay more attention to and develop your B players will directly help in retaining Millennials as well.

- **Make it clear that development is about growing in position as much as it is about moving on to the next promotion.** Even though many Millennials like to learn for the sake of learning, some are more focused on advancing in their careers than others. Remind these Millennials of the benefits of slowing down and focusing on learning as much as possible in their current roles.

  If a Millennial finds himself or herself assigned a task he or she thinks is too easy, the employee should be challenged to see how strong a performance can be given in that position, while at the same time learning as much as possible. Think of it as increasing the level of difficulty, pushing Millennials to perform at a higher level. The challenge is how well can they do?

  You can remind them that the best way to audition for a new, higher position is to outperform in their current role—and the more they outperform, the better. Encourage them to coach and mentor their colleagues who aren't doing as well, and so on. There is typically more employees can do to improve their performance and contribution in their current role.

- **Provide sabbaticals.** One way to give your Millennials opportunities to develop is to let them get that development outside of the organization through an employee sabbatical.[1] A number of organizations use sabbaticals to give their employees a chance to take a break from their day-to-day routines, recharge their batteries, and expand their learning and experience through entirely different activities. A sabbatical can be either paid or unpaid, and can range from a few weeks to a number of months. In some cases, the sabbatical is restricted to activities like education or working with charitable organizations, while in others, there are no restrictions.

Sabbaticals typically are limited to people with a minimum numbers of years of tenure, but that does not necessarily make them unattractive to Millennials—and they may help you retain Millennials who want to take advantage of that benefit. While the typical sabbatical appears to be relatively short (no more than two months), if a down cycle or recession hits, you can put temporarily redundant but still highly valued employees on extended unpaid or partially funded sabbaticals (six months or longer). Doing this can keep Millennials engaged and ready to come back to work for you while they benefit from learning and contributing in other venues over an extended period of time.

Pay

Pay today is more transparent than it's ever been before. In the past, companies tried to keep pay information confidential and many mostly succeeded. Employees only had side conversations in hallways and among friends and family. That era is long gone. Anyone with a computer or smartphone is a few clicks or taps away from publicly posted information on how much jobs like theirs pay—and often how much other people working in the same organization are paid. The question is not whether Millennials will find information about their pay from nontraditional sources; it's what the sources of that information will be and how accurate they are. The more transparent you can be about your organization's pay practices, the better.

Millennials are motivated to work and want to be paid well for it. They especially don't believe they should have to take a pay cut just because their organization might contribute to the community. Pay them what they are worth, and don't shortchange them.

Millennials have real financial needs. They aren't just spoiled brats who want more money. They are concerned about paying the bills, reducing debt, and saving for retirement. They struggle with financial issues that affect their job and career choices. So quibbling with them to save a few pennies can backfire really quickly.

Ultimately, how Millennials feel about their pay cannot be separated from what they are being asked to do. If the work demands are reasonable and pay is adequate, everything may be just fine. If the work demands are very high, then pay has to be higher to compensate. But pay alone is not enough. Even if you pay premium compensation rates because you have very high productivity standards, the entire package will be what matters. Do they see a longer-term future working with you? Is there the opportunity for advancement? Are they shown appreciation for their hard work? Do they like their teammates and bosses? Is the work interesting and meaningful? All these factors and more combine to create the full package that dictates how Millennials feel about their pay and about working for you.

Actions to Take

- **Understand that compensation first and foremost pays the bills.** Millennials are often dealing with difficult financial situations, so the amount in the pay package matters to them in real, tangible ways. It doesn't matter if their financial difficulties are due to circumstances beyond their control or choices they made. The reality they face is just that—reality. If they don't earn enough to pay back student loans, get ahead of their bills, and address their concerns about saving for the future, they will be distracted, have a hard time committing themselves fully at work, and look for someplace else to work that can offer them greater compensation. They may not leave immediately, but the risk of them leaving will be higher than if they are well paid.

- **Understand that compensation is also a measure of value and self-worth.** You may have made less money at the same stage in your career. Or you may have made more. You may believe

Millennials are paid just fine relative to what they can get elsewhere or relative to other people doing the same jobs who have longer tenure with the organization. But what matters to Millennials is how they feel about their pay, not whether management thinks they are paid fairly.

Pay sends a very powerful signal regarding how the organization feels about Millennials, and it affects how Millennials feel about themselves. Think about how you would feel about yourself if you truly believed that you were seriously underpaid. It would affect your feelings of self-worth. Millennials are no different.

- **You can underpay or overwork, not both.** You can underpay people you don't work very hard, and you can overwork people you pay really well. But you can't underpay and overwork employees for very long before they'll decide to go somewhere else. Millennials are willing to work very hard, but they expect to be paid well for it. If they are working very hard, they may feel undervalued even at above-average pay rates, because compensation is really about the total package of work and pay.

- **Seize control of the conversation about pay back from the Internet.** Pay transparency is increased by what's available online, but the quality of the information can be very poor. If you don't provide information about pay, Millennials will have only what they can find online and from talking with their friends to inform their opinions about their pay. The more information and detail you can provide, the more they will trust what you say, and the less they will rely on (arguably less accurate) online postings.

  Be honest with the compensation information you provide. Employees will certainly check what they are told against what can be found online and will be quick to note discrepancies.

- **Pay is about the whole package, not just the amount on the paycheck.** For Millennials, compensation isn't just how much shows up in their pay packets every two or four weeks. It is also about their development, how appreciated they are made to feel through nonmonetary means, how much they are expected to work, how much flexibility they have, whether they see taking less now as paying back over time, and so on. The entire package of workload, stress, long-term outcomes, and pay has to make sense to the Millennials or they will feel a need to look elsewhere for a better deal.

Putting It All Together

This chapter has provided some very specific recommendations on how to engage Millennials in the areas of people, work, and opportunities. If you can do all of them, you will be as successful with Millennials as anyone could ever expect. But maybe you can't do everything. You have to prioritize based on your organization's situation and first change the things that you believe will give you the greatest return. With that in mind, we offer some key points that might help you think through how to focus and prioritize.

"Aside from the people, the hours, the work, the pay, the stress and the migraines, this is the best job I ever had."

© Randy Glasbergen, glasbergen.com

1. Millennials will leave if their needs aren't met.

Make sure that the organization provides Millennials a complete package that addresses their professional and personal needs, one that includes promotion, advancement, workload, development, community, appreciation, and pay. The more complete the package, the greater your chances of not only attracting and retaining them but also of winning their engagement and commitment.

2. Millennials can leave—but they don't necessarily want to.

Unless they are in a bad situation, most Millennials don't leave just for the sake of being somewhere else. They leave to escape a bad situation or to level up to a substantially better one. Change is no easier for Millennials than it is for anyone else, and they want to stay if things can work out as they'd like them to.

3. Sharing their values is as much about compensation and interesting work as it is about doing good.

Be a good corporate citizen—but don't expect them to think it makes up for deficiencies in compensation or opportunities. Millennials want to be part of organizations that are making positive contributions to society in whatever ways they can that are both effective and appropriate for the industry and business model. This is a "both/and" situation. Millennials want to see positive contributions to society from their employer, but not at the expense of what they want and feel they deserve for their compensation and their careers.

4. Recognize and help millennials manage the real financial pressures they are under by providing them with good options.

Acknowledging the pressures and providing ways for Millennials to manage their financial lives will help build their commitment to staying and working hard to help your organization succeed. Many Millennials are operating under strong financial pressures: student debt, mortgage debt, a future with meager or nonexistent pensions, and long-term economic uncertainty. The financial circumstances of members of older generations vary greatly from person to person, even among those working side by side in the same job; the situation for Millennials is no different.

Afterword

As you finish reading this chapter, you may be saying to yourself, *Many of the ideas and recommendations you've developed based on your studies of Millennials such as pay transparency, feedback, opportunity, and community could apply to employees of any age.* You're right. Employees of all ages benefit when managers and organizations implement the recommendations we've discussed.

CHAPTER 7

LOOKING TO
THE FUTURE

Millennials will age, just like the rest of us. Along with that aging process come different life stages and a shift in concerns that will continue to affect Millennials' choices and the organizations that employ them for about the next 40 years.

We can't predict the future. However, we can look at current research and the past experiences of other generations to suggest what organizations should be thinking about and planning for with regard to Millennials in the future. Our conclusions and recommendations are based on a combination of human patterns of behavior that have been well established by research and what we know about the trends in society now.

Whether our predictions actually play out will depend on difficult-to-foresee events in technology, politics, the global economy, and so on. For example, people in the 1950s predicted that we would commute by individual car-airplane hybrids by 2000; that didn't exactly work out. On the other hand, the comic strip *Dick Tracy* had a two-way wrist radio in the 1940s, and in the 1960s the television cartoon *The Jetsons* had video calls and the television show *Star Trek* had handheld communicators that allowed people to talk across the world. But nobody predicted wrist and handheld telephones and videoconferencing with people around the world that is virtually free.

Will the cost of solar-generated energy drop tenfold, or will fusion energy be achieved? Will global warming accelerate and raise sea levels worldwide by 15 feet? Will a transporter (à la *Star Trek*) be developed and change transportation altogether? Most likely, people will continue to muddle through and adapt as best they can to changing conditions. On that presumption, here are the areas we believe will be particularly important for organizations to pay attention to in the near future.

Trends Affecting Millennials Long Term

Starting a Career During a Recession Depresses Total Career Earnings

One widely discussed but not well-understood phenomenon in economics is the long-term effects of the labor market conditions people experience when they are young. A large part of the Millennial generation has come of age during an era encompassing two very different economic environments: the moderate growth of the early 2000s followed by the Great Recession of 2007, the effects of which will take many years to play out.

The research on the long-term impact of starting work during an economic downturn indicates that people who enter the labor market during economic hard times make less than those who start during an economic boom for at least a decade, if not longer.[1] Why? In a difficult economy, there are fewer good jobs to choose from. The jobs that people are able to find when they enter the workforce don't pay as well or offer the same breadth of developmental opportunities as the jobs available in a growing economy. Therefore they start at lower pay in a less optimal job, and that starting point can affect the rest of their career.

Just as the generations that lived through the Great Depression carried economic lessons with them for the rest of their lives, we expect to see the impact of the Great Recession on Millennials' economic options and decisions persist for many, many years.[2] At the same time, we know that how this will affect the life and career of individual Millennials is a result of their particular circumstances, such as precisely when they entered the workforce.

For example, in the United States, the United Kingdom, and Europe, the oldest Millennials (born 1980–1982) graduated university during the middle of the economic expansion of the early to mid-2000s. By the time the Great Recession hit these countries, many of this group had already established themselves in viable career paths and were able to survive the cutbacks and layoffs that were rampant in the late 2000s. Their younger counterparts, the middle of the Millennial generation who graduated in 2007 to 2010 and beyond, have had a much harder time. And the youngest Millennials, those born from 1995 to 2000, haven't even graduated university yet (we have not included them in the research reported here) and will have equally unique conditions facing them in the working world.[3]

The bottom line is that the Great Recession matters and will have a lasting impact on many members of the Millennial generation for many years to come. But that applies primarily to the Millennials who started their careers during those dark years and less to the oldest and youngest Millennials.

Millennials Will Live Longer and Be Less Economically Secure in Retirement

Millennials worry about their retirement security because they face long lives after age 65 and greater uncertainty about how their retirement will be funded.

People are living longer, which challenges traditional ideas of the right age to retire. When government-run public pension programs were established decades ago, life expectancy was much shorter than it is today. In 1940, men who lived to be 65 were predicted to live an additional 12.7 years (to age 77.7), and women an additional 14.7 years (to age 79.7).[4] That meant that most people could expect to spend only 13 to 15 years drawing a public pension. Today in the United States, life expectancy for both men and women has increased, to age 84.3 for men and age 86.6 for women.[5] People living longer while continuing to retire at the same age as before has resulted in both public and private pension programs having to pay out more than had been anticipated when they were established. The question currently being debated is how to pay for retirement, as there are concerns about whether the current programs are sustainable in the long run, and at what level.[6,7]

In the United States, there is a long-term trend away from defined benefit to defined contribution retirement plans, which has shifted risk about having enough—and saving enough—for retirement away from organizations and onto employees. Part of the problem with this shift is that people typically don't like to defer happiness today for happiness in some distant future and therefore don't save enough for retirement. While Millennials may reverse this trend,[8] having enough saved for retirement is a big concern for them.

"It's the new man - he wants to know what the company retirement plan is."

Source: www.businesscartoonshop.com

Another issue with privately financed and managed retirement accounts is business cycle risk. The greatest returns over time for retirement portfolios are available through the stock market. But what happens if the stock market falls substantially just before you are about to retire? Unless you've hedged your investments, you are faced with either retiring on schedule with a lower standard of living or delaying retirement until you can rebuild your savings. We saw an example of that in the United States during the Great Recession, with millions of Baby Boomers who had planned to retire unable to because their retirement savings were cut substantially when the stock market plunged. The Millennials who saw the impact of the stock market decline on their elders' retirement accounts are quite aware of what can happen. It is likely that this memory will last for a very long time, affecting how they perceive self-financed retirement plans.

Though they are understandably concerned about retirement, Millennials face unprecedented longevity and vitality—living to much older ages and being healthier—than the generations that came before them. So they may *want* to work for more years, creating a pool of experienced workers who can continue to contribute for years beyond what is now the traditional retirement age. We fully expect Millennials will challenge longstanding norms about what work looks like at older ages, trends that are only now starting to emerge as many Baby Boomers have entered the traditional age of retirement but have not retired.

For Most Millennials, There Is Not Going to Be a Pot of Gold at the End of the Career Rainbow

While global poverty has been reduced over the past four decades, the United States, the United Kingdom, and many other industrialized societies have had increases in within-group inequality.[9] This means that among groups of people who have similar education or who work in the same field or occupation, the differences between the winners and (relative) losers grew larger. The wages of college-educated workers also have been affected by the proliferation of the Internet and high-speed communications, which allow knowledge work that used to stay within national borders to be shopped around the world to the lowest bidder. Many traditionally safe knowledge-work occupations such as law, accounting, architecture, and laboratory technology have seen increased pressure on both wages and jobs, leading to lower raises and greater economic uncertainty for college-educated workers—our Millennial focus here—than has been seen in over half a century.

Does this mean Millennials should abandon hopes of having fulfilling careers? No. But they shouldn't expect to find a pot of gold at the end of the career rainbow either. Of course a minority will do extremely well, but that's precisely the point: only a small group of Millennials can realistically expect to hit the financial jackpot in their careers. Assuming the current trajectory and policies hold, many will have to be content with some financial insecurity and maybe financial comfort, rather than substantial wealth.

The High Cost of Education Reduces Choices

Spending on education and student debt is a real issue for many Millennials and their families. In the United States, the cost of college continues to increase faster than inflation.[10] As a consequence, Millennials are graduating with more student debt than ever, and the trend isn't looking positive. Debt from their own education choices and career challenges will increase the strain Millennials feel as parents, at a time when they want to provide the best opportunities for their own children.

With Millennials, it is possible that we are looking at a generation where large numbers may retire without having paid off their student loans: currently, there are more than two million retirees with outstanding student debt, and more than 11 percent of households in the 50–64-year-old group in 2010 had average outstanding education debt of $28,000.[11,12] The level of student debt is much greater for Millennials than for older generations, so unless there is a dramatic change in their prospects for earning a lot of money in their lifetimes (which is unlikely if current trends continue), it is likely that Millennials will enter retirement with the greatest levels of student debt ever.

Now consider these trends in light of the general economic trends. Millennials are facing rising education costs and student debt in a labor market where they cannot be assured that choosing a historically lucrative occupation will provide them with the financial outcomes they could have anticipated in the past. We foresee this creating increasing strain on Millennials as they set up their households and move on to their midcareer jobs.

Conclusion: Economic Issues

In today's global economy, no organization or job is secure, and people cannot count on career success, either in terms of the specific jobs and organizations they want to work for or the amount of money they want to earn (see earlier discussion). Many Millennials who started their careers with debt and during a recession continue to be affected by the lingering poor economy.

However, Millennials have grown up with no illusions that the world is any different than this. Previous generations came of age at a time when retirement was more secure (Baby Boomers) or was transitioning to a different system (Gen Xers). Millennials are the first generation to enter the workforce believing they have only themselves to rely on when it comes to retirement savings. They know they have to maintain an edge in the labor market to ensure their financial well-being. That's likely a main reason we found the strong emphasis we did among Millennials on learning and professional development. They know they need to grow their skills to survive.

Health Trends Affecting Millennials, Organizations, and Society Long Term

Millennials Have Been Identified as the Heaviest Generation to Date, Which Is Likely to Affect Their Long-Term Health

In 2012 in the United States, the obesity rate for teenagers was more than four times what it was in 1980.[13] In 2007, a survey found that two-thirds of U.S. students at the secondary level did not engage in enough physical activity, and three-quarters didn't have good eating habits (as defined by underconsumption of fruits and vegetables and overconsumption of soda).[14]

We bring up childhood behavior because the consequences of obesity developed in childhood manifest themselves in adulthood. Children who are obese are more likely to develop heart disease and high blood pressure.[15] People who are obese are more likely to become diabetic.[16] This isn't just a concern in economically more developed countries. Childhood obesity has also increased in the developing world,[17] and there are real concerns about the ubiquity of diabetes globally.[18]

Organizations should be concerned about an incoming employee population that is heavier than it was in the past. There is ample evidence that more money is spent on medical care when people are overweight.[19] In addition to higher healthcare costs, obesity has been shown to increase absenteeism and reduce wages.[20,21] In short, increases in obesity cost individuals, organizations, and societies. Obesity-related health issues can have substantial financial repercussions for individuals, organizations, and societies that pay for or subsidize healthcare.

Lest you think this is a first-world problem, here are a few data points. An article published in the *International Journal of Obesity* predicts that in 2030,[22] assuming past trends hold,

- 60 percent of people in China will be overweight, and 13 percent will be obese.
- 29 percent of people in India will be overweight, and 5 percent will be obese.
- 50 percent of people in other parts of Asia and the islands will be overweight, and 14 percent will be obese.
- 44 percent of people in Latin America and the Caribbean will be overweight, and 38 percent will be obese.
- 29 percent of people in Sub-Saharan Africa will be overweight, and 17 percent will be obese.
- 23 percent of people in the Middle Eastern Crescent will be overweight, and 24 percent will be obese.

This means that organizations and societies globally will be affected by obesity more than they have been in the past. They need to figure out how to address this issue, or they will end up paying for the outcomes.

Given the data we've seen, we have every reason to believe the trend will continue as Millennials age. This means that organizations need to start planning for this eventuality while working simultaneously to bend the curve away from this unpleasant future.

While everyone understands that these conditions are fundamentally the result of individual choices, organizations have an opportunity to make it easier and more beneficial for individuals to make healthy choices. For example, some organizations provide opportunities for their staff to get and stay fit through in-office gyms or gym memberships, healthy cafeteria options, specific exercise times, and incentives for demonstrating a healthy lifestyle. Some organizations have looked at the literature on shaping behavior and have started implementing such practices as hiding the less healthy snacks behind the more healthy snacks, putting water on display while making sugared drinks difficult to find, having people pay for food in the cafeteria by the weight of their food rather than the dish selected, and providing substantial discounts for more healthy choices.

Millennials spend a large percentage of their waking time at work. A workplace that makes healthy choices easier and more beneficial for Millennials as individuals will reap a return because they will be more fit, less expensive to employ, and appreciative of the care shown toward them.

A Sedentary Lifestyle Is a Health Concern

Another health concern for the foreseeable future is a decrease in physical activity. Many people live in a world where physical activity is minimized. Millennials (and other adults) in professional positions in organizations spend a large part of their day sitting— sitting at a computer, sitting in meetings, sitting at lunch.

People try to combat this by getting exercise. Some see the wearable tech trend as a move in the direction of increasing physical fitness. Even if it is, getting sufficient exercise isn't enough. While exercise is important, simply put, sitting too much is unhealthy, even with regular exercise.[23] As long as most work is done sitting down at a computer or desk, this is going to continue to be a concern for Millennials and the organizations they work for.

What can people do? Get up more frequently. Walk down the hall or to another floor to talk with someone rather than e-mailing, IMing, or calling. When on a conference call alone in your office, get up and walk in place, or see if you can take the call while on a treadmill or other exercise equipment. Set a reminder to encourage you to get up frequently rather than sitting in one place all day. Even if you aren't very active, getting up and walking around can improve your health.

Organizations need to encourage these activities and figure out how to organize work so it can be more active. Some organizations have walking meetings for small groups. Others set up treadmills in offices so people can work and walk at the same time. Some set tables at standing height rather than sitting and have desks that can be used standing as well as sitting. The specifics need to be based on a strong understanding of what will maximize employee health and the work flow within the organization simultaneously. Whatever the implementation plan, the desired outcome is the same: people need to move throughout the day more than they do now. This is a particular concern for Millennials who are entering the workforce heavier than any generation before them.

Stress Harms Physical and Mental Health

Stress is recognized as a significant global issue.[24] People everywhere are stressed, and a large portion of the stress is about work.

Studies conducted over the past few years in the United States clearly show that Millennials' stress levels are as high as those of older adults.[25,26] A study by the American Psychological Association shows that about one-third report feeling isolated, and almost as many say that their stress level has affected their physical and mental health.[27] Though they do engage in stress management techniques, those they choose tend toward sedentary behaviors (e.g., surfing the Internet, watching television or movies, napping, and eating), which do not support a healthy lifestyle as much as more physical ones do.[28]

The report also finds that parents are more stressed than are nonparents.[29] Given that the majority of Millennials are not yet parents, this is of considerable concern. If their stress levels are so bad now when they aren't parents, how much worse is it going to get when they become parents? Or will there be a tipping point after which stress will go down? It is impossible to tell, but it is something organizations need to keep an eye on.

We can't say for sure, but given the financial pressures Millennials are currently under and the increased financial stress having a family brings, including concerns about retirement, we expect Millennials' stress levels will increase. And too much stress, no matter where it comes from, has a negative effect on health, absenteeism, and productivity. Instituting practical, healthy workplace-based choices for reducing stress (e.g., gym memberships, exercise time, team sports) could help employees simultaneously improve their health, reduce their stress levels, and become more productive.

Conclusion: Health

The long-term health trajectory for Millennials is not as positive as it could be. But there is still time for organizations to shift the direction through concerted health initiatives focused on helping employees make healthy choices and improving their health outcomes. If Millennials' health improves, everyone benefits.

Societal Shifts

Society is shifting, pretty much everywhere. There is a trend toward Millennials getting married later and having children later. More Millennials are remaining single. More women are staying in the workplace after having children, and more men are taking on childcare responsibilities. All of these trends will affect organizations because people's home lives affect their work lives, and vice versa.

Millennials Form Families Later, Which Impacts the Timing of Their Career Flexibility

There is a shift toward later marriage around the world.[30] In the United States, Millennials are getting married later, buying homes later, and having children later.[31] This results in increased flexibility in their early career years—flexibility to take more risks, work more hours, change jobs when they don't like them, take advantage of opportunities overseas, and so on. This extended flexibility can translate into good news for organizations: Millennials early in their careers will have more latitude to move to other places and try other jobs without worrying about disrupting the lives of a spouse and/or a child.

However, Millennials' increased flexibility early in their careers will be balanced by less flexibility later on. The go-getting, single twenty-somethings (and early thirty-somethings) will become people in their late thirties and forties who want more time to spend with young children, just as they are reaching levels in the organization with substantially greater job demands and responsibilities. Organizations that want to keep the best and brightest Millennials must be prepared to be flexible in their career demands. They need to work with Millennials to come up with career paths for middle and upper management positions that don't require employees to give up their family life.

An Increase in Singleness Will Increase Career Flexibility for Some Employees

Fewer Millennials are choosing to get married than people in past generations did, and it is likely that some of those who do get married will subsequently get divorced. That means that there will be many employees who don't have responsibilities to a spouse. This is an issue for organizations to keep an eye on because it has implications for hours worked, mobility later in a career, and an increased importance in creating a community at work that Millennials can be a part of as they grow older.

The good news for organizations is that this new cadre of unattached workers and managers may be prepared to give their all to work, or at least have more flexibility than their peers who have family obligations. However, organizations need to manage the dynamics here carefully for two reasons. First, from an equity standpoint, promotion policies that favor unattached people seem churlish and insensitive, as well as possibly providing grounds for class-action lawsuits. Everyone knows it's possible to create more family-friendly alternatives, including providing more flexible options for when and where work gets done and allowing employees to take a break from career advancement to spend more time with family (hitting the pause button on career advancement).

Second, unattached Millennials will resent having to do more of the work simply because their colleagues with families have other obligations outside work. Even single people have interests outside work that they feel strongly about. So taking away their ability to enjoy their out-of-work pursuits simply because you're trying to support their coworkers who have families runs the risk of driving them away. If you take the time and effort to design and implement options that work for your organization and all Millennials—attached or otherwise—you will be rewarded for not taking the easy road.

An Increase in Single-Parent Households and Two-Career Families Will Increase Demands on Organizations to Be Responsive to Their Needs

There is a global trend toward an increase in single-parent households in many economically developed countries.[32] Whether a result of divorce, the choice to have a child as a single parent, or the death of a spouse, single-parent households are more common than they were 20 years ago. There is also a trend toward two-career families, as more women than in the past return to work after having a child. In some cases, it is a desire; in others, a financial necessity.

Regardless of whether it's single-parent households or two-career families, the issues organizations need to consider are very similar. Organizations need to be aware of the responsibilities of working parents with children and devise ways to help them manage their responsibilities at work and at home, such as providing better benefits and greater ability to choose when and where work gets done. Policies should benefit as large a group of employees as possible, not just one group or another. When policies about childcare and flexible work arrangements are highly tailored toward a specific group, they run the risk of losing the support of everyone else, either through apathy ("It doesn't apply to me, so why should I care?") or antipathy ("Why is that group getting special treatment and I'm not?"). Either way, a bigger umbrella that covers more people is always better whenever possible.

Millennial Women

While it is likely that many Millennials will have two-career households, a segment of that population is finding it increasingly difficult to have a career and manage children at the same time. Research by Harvard Business School[33] and the Pew Research Center[34] indicates that Millennial women may be more likely than were Gen X women to take time away from work so they can meet their family responsibilities. Millennial women don't believe they can simultaneously maintain the career they want while also meeting their responsibilities to their families. Therefore, some choose to step away from the career ladder for a few years and return later. Organizations that can implement policies that make it easier for them to stay or to return will reap the benefits of a highly engaged and motivated workforce.

Greater Connectivity in Their Personal Lives May Make Employees More Mobile for Work

It is likely that Millennials will have greater mobility throughout their lives than previous generations. With technology more prevalent and able to help people keep in touch, it is easier to move to other cities, countries, or continents and still keep up with friends and family.

Millennials are particularly good at staying in touch with loved ones, even if they don't get to see them in person. That skill gives them the flexibility to be highly mobile because they bring their friends and family with them electronically wherever they go. The good news for organizations is that this fits well with a world where work is done ever more by people in far-flung locations who work together virtually.

Conclusion: Societal Shifts

When people have children and there is no caregiver permanently stationed at home, there is additional stress on the parents to manage the flow of day-to-day life. School drop-offs and pick-ups, school holidays, school events, sick children, and so on can interrupt the workday and may interfere with the possibility of an employee working extended hours for the organization. Most school systems in most countries don't have hours that mimic the workday of busy professionals, their vacation schedules don't perfectly match organizations' holiday schedules, and in-school activities where parents need to be present happen during school hours, which are the same as work hours. Kids get sick, and someone has to look after them. While some families have a parent who stays home or help in the form of a paid childcare professional, a relative, or a friend, not all working parents do.

Given the trend toward an increasing number of single-parent households and dual-career couples with children, organizations need to figure out—quickly—how to accommodate people's lives, because these challenges aren't going away. Organizations can no longer assume someone other than their employee can stay home when a child gets sick or other family needs arise because, with increasing frequency, the one who has to stay home is the employee. Many offer a great deal of flexibility, allowing employees to work from home to accommodate family needs.

Afterword: What About the Next Generation— Those Born after 2000?

People frequently ask us what the next generation is going to be like and what organizations should do to prepare for them. (One of us is particularly interested because her son was born in 2008.) The answer is: we don't know for sure. Nobody does, because the oldest of that generation are currently 16 years of age, and the majority are under 10. We don't know what types of economic conditions they'll face, how social norms will change, or what technologies they'll have access to. We don't even know what they'll be called. Some have called this next cohort Generation Z. Others have suggested iGen, post-Millennials, and more. We don't know what name will ultimately stick, but we do have some ideas about what can and cannot be said about them.

"What's so new about all this? I've never trusted anyone over thirty, under thirty, or thirty."

Source: Whitney Darrow, Jr./The New Yorker Collection/The Cartoon Bank

What we do know, based on all of our work studying generations, is that by the time they get to the workplace, they'll care about who they work with, having work to do that they enjoy and find meaningful, and having the opportunity and compensation to build the kind of life they want to live.

Hopefully, by the time the next generation starts entering the workforce, organizations will have shifted enough to make more of what they want possible. Regardless of what happens, we plan to keep an eye on them and report back when we have a better idea of the particulars of what they want, what they need, and how organizations need to manage and lead them.

Until then, we wish you the best of luck in managing all of the generations in your workplace. Remember, the more solutions you can find that work for both employees of all generations and for the organization, the better off everyone will be . . . including you!

ACKNOWLEDGMENTS

We would like to thank everyone who contributed to the writing of this book, both directly and indirectly. Many of our colleagues, friends, and family provided their time freely, reading chapters, providing feedback, and sharing stories with us. A very large number of both Millennials and older people around the world participated in interviews and focus groups that provided the context that made the data come to life. And a much larger group of people participated in the multiple survey efforts that collected the data. Special thank yous go out to our colleagues at the Center for Effective Organizations and Center for Creative Leadership who directly contributed to the surveys and data collection efforts that are the foundation on which the book was developed, and to editors and other staff at McGraw-Hill who worked tirelessly to make this book happen (especially Casey Ebro, Ann Pryor, Daina Penikas, and Ishita Bhatnagar).

We would like to extend a special thank you to PwC for providing extensive support for work that contributed to this book. PwC and its global leadership team have been true thought partners in helping us improve our understanding of what the Millennial generation wants and needs from the world of work. We owe a particular debt of gratitude to Anne Donovan, Bianca Martorella, Nora Wu, Julie Gordon, and Dennis Finn.

We would like to specifically thank the following people, in no particular order, for their contributions to the book: Nora Hilton, Aaron Griffith, Alice Mark, Lorelei Palacpac, George Benson, Maritza Salazar, Sue Mohrman, Sarah Stawiski, Marian Ruderman, Bill Gentry, Laura Graves, Todd Weber, Kristin Cullen, David Berke, Maura Stevenson, Philip Koekemoer, Jean Leslie, David Altman, Jennifer Martineau, Emily Hoole, Pete Scisco, David Powell, Stephen Martin, Portia Mount, Kevin O'Gorman, Jeremy Hirshberg, Kim Warmbier, Linda David, Anne Fithern, Val Kroenke,

Wendy Hawkins, David Hawkins, Natalie Hawkins, Margie Weit-kamp, Gary Weitkamp, Stephanie Trovas, Eric Stromberg, Susan Tardanico, Becky Launder, Jennifer Habig, Julie Min Chayet, Emilie Petrone, Alison Gurganus, Katharine Newman, Katherine Wisz, Kali Patterson, Kirsten Poehlmann Kung, Barbara Troupin, Andrea Papanastassiou, Alex Papanastassiou, Teri Papanastassiou, Dimitri Papanastassiou, David Dickter, Kristen Boyle, Steve Hunt, Angela Pratt, Aaron Lamb, Jennifer Mueller, and David Whitehead.

As we mentioned in the Introduction, this book would not have been written without the support and assistance of everyone listed here. In addition, there are hundreds of others not listed who helped in smaller though no less important ways. We are grateful to you all. If you like what you read in this book, we owe much of the credit to these people and more. If you don't like what you read, blame us!

APPENDICES

Appendix I.1

MILLENNIAL ORGANIZATIONAL LEVELS (BY COUNTRY)

COUNTRY	ADMINISTRATIVE/ NONPROFESSIONAL	PROFESSIONAL	FIRST-LEVEL MANAGER	MID-LEVEL MANAGER	DIRECTOR/ EXECUTIVE
Brazil	8%	52%	25%	14%	1%
Canada	6%	29%	40%	21%	4%
China (including Hong Kong/Macau)	9%	44%	33%	13%	2%
France	2%	24%	51%	21%	1%
Germany	7%	66%	20%	6%	1%
India	4%	54%	32%	9%	2%
Italy	8%	56%	29%	7%	0.2%
Japan	2%	55%	37%	6%	1%
Korea	1%	47%	46%	6%	0.3%
Mexico	3%	36%	50%	11%	1%
Netherlands	8%	32%	46%	14%	0.4%
Russia	9%	36%	33%	15%	7%
Singapore	1%	39%	41%	19%	1%
South Africa	3%	43%	34%	14%	7%
Spain	4%	41%	46%	9%	1%
Switzerland (including Lichtenstein)	18%	41%	24%	16%	2%
Taiwan	4%	51%	34%	10%	1%
United Kingdom	3%	38%	35%	19%	5%
United States	1%	48%	32%	16%	3%

Appendix I.2

MILLENNIAL GENDER (BY COUNTRY)

COUNTRY	MALE	FEMALE
Brazil	53%	47%
Canada	42%	58%
China (including Hong Kong/Macau)	34%	66%
France	48%	52%
Germany	55%	45%
India	68%	32%
Italy	53%	47%
Japan	77%	23%
Korea	67%	33%
Mexico	56%	44%
Netherlands	62%	38%
Russia	39%	61%
Singapore	37%	63%
South Africa	47%	53%
Spain	60%	40%
Switzerland (including Lichtenstein)	51%	49%
Taiwan	28%	72%
United Kingdom	51%	49%
United States	50%	50%

Appendix I.3

MILLENNIAL MARITAL STATUS AND CHILDREN (BY COUNTRY)

COUNTRY	MARRIED	HAVE CHILDREN
Brazil	18%	9%
Canada	25%	8%
China (including Hong Kong/Macau)	25%	8%
France	21%	12%
Germany	14%	5%
India	36%	12%
Italy	8%	3%
Japan	31%	10%
Korea	23%	9%
Mexico	16%	11%
Netherlands	16%	10%
Russia	37%	18%
Singapore	17%	4%
South Africa	30%	15%
Spain	14%	4%
Switzerland (including Lichtenstein)	17%	3%
Taiwan	9%	3%
United Kingdom	21%	7%
United States	31%	13%

Appendix 1.1

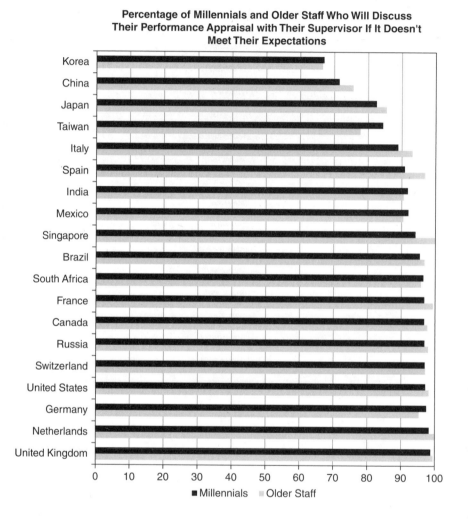

Percentage of Millennials and Older Staff Who Will Discuss Their Performance Appraisal with Their Supervisor If It Doesn't Meet Their Expectations

Appendix 1.2

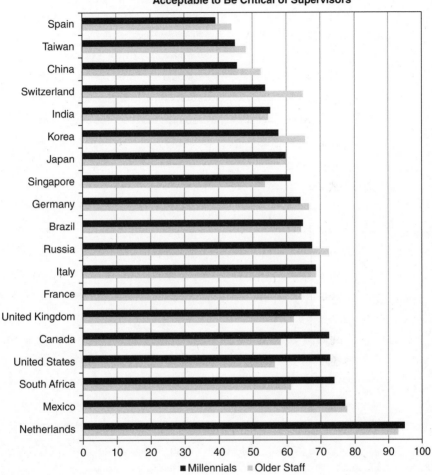

Percentage of Millennials and Older Staff Who Say It Is Acceptable to Be Critical of Supervisors

Appendix 3.1

PERCENTAGE WHO DISCUSS THEIR COMPENSATION WITH THEIR COWORKERS (BY COUNTRY)

COUNTRY	MILLENNIALS	OLDER STAFF
Brazil	58%	30%
Canada	44%	15%
China (including HK/Macau)	44%	21%
France	75%	54%
Germany	32%	18%
India	18%	15%
Italy	59%	38%
Japan	46%	22%
Korea	39%	29%
Mexico	44%	32%
Netherlands	54%	47%
Russia	38%	17%
Singapore	34%	23%
South Africa	36%	15%
Spain	55%	33%
Switzerland (including Lichtenstein)	41%	29%
Taiwan	21%	4%
United Kingdom	41%	18%
United States	29%	9%

Appendix 4.1

Millennials' Beliefs About What Makes a Good Manager or Leader

- 80 percent of Millennials believe that good leaders are considerate and kind.
- 83 percent believe that good leaders are willing to use their time to help others.
- 78 percent believe that good leaders care about the needs and feelings of others.
- 89 percent believe getting to know fellow workers well should be important to a manager.
- 80 percent believe that developing close ties with coworkers should be important to a manager.
- 88 percent believe that forming relationships with coworkers should be important to a manager.
- 84 percent say their immediate supervisors should go out of their way to help team members when things get demanding at work.
- 89 percent believe that good leaders deal with conflicts among group members in constructive ways.
- 90 percent believe that good leaders encourage group members to work together.
- 89 percent believe that good leaders encourage collaborative behavior among team members.
- 91 percent believe that good leaders are enthusiastic in a way that inspires commitment.
- 90 percent believe that a good leader inspires and motivates others.
- 89 percent believe that good leaders motivate others to strive for excellence.
- 89 percent believe that a good leader communicates a vision others can relate to.

Appendix 5.1

Millennials' Perception of Organizational Politics

- 25 percent of Millennials believe that people in their organization build themselves up by tearing others down.
- 36 percent believe there is an influential group that no one ever crosses.
- 24 percent believe that promotions don't mean anything because they are so political.
- 32 percent believe it is safer to think what you are told than to make up your own mind.
- 36 percent believe that agreeing with powerful others is the best option.
- 34 percent believe that it's best to not rock the boat.
- 20 percent believe they are not encouraged to speak out even when being critical of well-established ideas.
- 49 percent believe it is easier to remain quiet than to fight the system.
- 26 percent don't believe that good ideas are desired if it means disagreeing with superiors.
- 28 percent believe that in their organization telling others what they want to hear is often better than telling the truth.

REFERENCES AND SUGGESTED READING

Achieve Guidance (2013). *The Millennial Impact Research: The 2013 Millennial Impact Report.* Retrieved from http://cdn.trustedpartner .com/docs/library/AchieveMCON2013/Research%20Report/ Millennial%20Impact%20Research.pdf

American Psychological Association (2014). *Stress in America: Are Teens Adopting Adults' Stress Habits?* Retrieved from https://www.apa.org/ news/press/releases/stress/2013/stress-report.pdf

American Psychological Association (2015). *Stress in America: Paying with Our Health.* Retrieved from http://www.apa.org/news/press/ releases/stress/2014/stress-report.pdf

Atkinson, A. B., Piketty, T., and Saez, E. (2011). Top Incomes in the Long Run of History. *Journal of Economic Literature,* 49(1), 3–71.

Barkin, S. L., Heerman, W. J., Warren, M. D., and, Rennhoff, C. (2010). Millennials and the world of work: The impact of obesity on health and productivity. *Journal of Business and Psychology,* 25(2), 239–245.

Bauerlein, M. (2008). *The Dumbest Generation: How the Digital Age Stupefies Young Americans and Jeopardizes our Future (or, Don't Trust Anyone Under 30).* London, England: Tarcher/Penguin Press.

Baum, C. L., II, and Ford, W. F. (2004). The Wage Effects of Obesity: A Longitudinal Study. *Health Economics,* 3(9), 885–899. Retrieved from http://amosyang.net/wp-content/uploads/2012/10/wageobesity.pdf

Billones, C. L. (2013, March 18). Japanese students deep in debt with $5 billion in loans. *JDP.* Retrieved from http://japandailypress.com/ japanese-students-deep-in-debt-with-5-billion-in-loans-1825368/

Blanchard, K., and Johnson, S. (2003). *The One Minute Manager.* New York: William Morrow.

Blanchflower, D. G., and Oswald, A. J. (2008). Is well-being U-shaped over the life cycle? *Social Science and Medicine,* 66(8) (April), 1733–1749.

Centers for Disease Control and Prevention (2014). *Child Obesity Facts. Obesity in Adolescents Aged 12–19 Increased from 5% in 1980 to 21% in 2012.* Retrieved February 10, 2015, from http://www.cdc.gov/ healthyyouth/obesity/facts.htm

Chura, H. (2006, April 22). Sabbaticals Aren't Just for Academics Anymore. *New York Times.* Retrieved from http://www.nytimes.com/2006/04/22/business/22sabbaticals.html

The College Board (2014). *Trends in College Pricing 2014.* Retrieved from http://trends.collegeboard.org/college-pricing

Collins, J. (2011). *Good to Great.* New York: HarperCollins Publishers.

Covey, S. M. R. (2006). *The Speed of Trust: The One Thing That Changes Everything.* New York: Free Press.

Deal, J. J. (2007). *Retiring the Generation Gap: How Employees Young and Old Can Find Common Ground.* New York: John Wiley& Sons.

Deal, J. J., Stawiski, S., Graves, L., Gentry, W. A., Weber, T. J., and Ruderman, M. (2013). Motivation at Work: Which Matters More, Generation or Managerial Level? *Consulting Psychology Journal,* 65(1) (March), 1–16.

Deloitte Touche Tohmatsu Ltd. (2014). Big demands and high expectations: What generation Y wants from business, government, and the future workplace. Retrieved January 21, 2014, from http://www2.deloitte.com/uk/en/pages/press-releases/articles/big-demands-and-high-expectations-what-generation-y-wants.html.

Feldman, D. (2013). Inspiring the Next Generation Workforce: The 2013 Millennial Impact Report. Achieve Guidance. Retrieved from http://*cdn.trustedpartner.com/docs/library/AchieveMCON2013/Research%20Report/Millennial%20Impact%20Research.pdf*

Finkelstein E., Fiebelkorn C., and Wang, G. (2005). The Costs of Obesity Among Full-Time Employees. *American Journal of Health Promotion,* 20(1), 45–51.

Gannon, M. J., and Demler, J. W. (1971). Organizational Level and Job Attitudes. *Psychological Reports,* 29, 399–402. Retrieved from http://www.amsciepub.com/doi/pdf/10.2466/pro.1971.29.2.399

Gardner, P. (2007). *Parental Involvement in the College Recruiting Process: To What Extent?* Retrieved from Michigan State University, Collegiate Employment Research Institute, Research Brief 2-2007, http://ceri.msu.edu/publications/pdf/ceri2-07.pdf

The Goldman Sachs Group, Inc. (2014). Millennials: The Housing Edition. In *Thematic Research.* Retrieved August 4, 2014, from http://www.thehousingrenaissance.com/resources/2014/Millennials_The_Housing_Edition_handout.pdf

Gottschalk, P., and Joyce, M. (1998). Cross-national Differences in the Rise in Earnings Inequality: Market and Institutional Factors. *The Review of Economics and Statistics,* 80(4), 489–502.

Harvard Business School (2015). *Life & Leadership After HBS: Findings.* Retrieved from http://www.hbs.edu/women50/docs/L_and_L_Survey_2Findings_12final.pdf

Hofschneider, A. (2013, September 10). Should You Bring Mom and Dad to the Office? Employers are Embracing the Involvement of Parents to Attract and Hold On to Talent. *Wall Street Journal*. Retrieved from http://www.wsj.com/articles/SB10001424127887323864604579066964214209866

Hossain, P., Kawar B., and El Nahas, M. (2007). Obesity and Diabetes in the Developing World—a Growing Challenge. *New England Journal of Medicine*, 356(3), 213–215.

The Institute for College Access & Success (2014, November). *Student Debt and the Class of 2013*. Retrieved from http://ticas.org/sites/default/files/legacy/fckfiles/pub/classof2013.pdf

Kahn, L. B. (2010). The long-term labor market consequences of graduating from college in a bad economy. *Labour Economics*, 17(2), 303–316.

Kelly, T., Yang, W., Chen, C.-S., Reynolds, K., and He, J. (2008). Global Burden of Obesity in 2005 and Projections to 2030. *International Journal of Obesity*, 32, 1431–1437. Retrieved from http://www.nature.com/ijo/journal/v32/n9/full/ijo2008102a.html

King, S. N., Altman, D. G., and Lee, R. J. (2011). *Discovering the Leader in You: How to Realize Your Leadership Potential*. Hoboken, NJ: John Wiley & Sons.

Lemieux, T. (2006). Increasing Residual Wage Inequality: Composition Effects, Noisy Data, or Rising Demand for Skill?" *American Economic Review*, 96(3), 461–498.

Levenson, A. (2006). Trends in Job and Wages in the U.S. Economy. In Lawler, E. E., and O'Toole, J., eds., *America at work: Choices and Challenges*, 87–107. New York: Palgrave MacMillan.

Levenson, A. (2010). Millennials and the World of Work. *Journal of Business and Psychology*, 25(2), 257–264.

Lorin, J. (2014, November 12). College Tuition in the U.S. Again Rises Faster Than Inflation. *Bloomberg Business*. Retrieved from http://www.bloomberg.com/news/articles/2014-11-13/college-tuition-in-the-u-s-again-rises-faster-than-inflation

McGill, H. C., Jr., McMahan, C.A., and Gidding, S. S. (2008). Preventing Heart Disease in the 21st Century: Implications of the Pathobiological Determinants of Atherosclerosis in Youth (PDAY) study. *Circulation*, 117(9), 1216–1227.

McHugh, D. (2013). The Convergence Of 3 Factors Is Driving A Worldwide Retirement Crisis. Retrieved from http://www.businessinsider.com/worldwide-retirement-crisis-coming-2013-12

Mishel, L., Bernstein, J., and Allegretto, S. (2005). *The State of Working America 2004/2005*. Ithaca, NY: ILR Press.

Olson, E. (2014, September 13). Student Loan Debt Burdens More Than Just Young People. *New York Times*. Retrieved from http://www.nytimes

.com/2014/09/13/business/student-loan-debt-burdens-more-than-just-young-people.html

Oreopoulos, P., von Wachter, T., and Heisz, A. (2006, April). The Short- and Long-Term Career Effects of Graduating in a Recession: Hysteresis and Heterogeneity in the Market for College Graduates. *National Bureau of Economic Research Working Paper*, no. 12159. Retrieved from http://www.nber.org/papers/w12159

Owen, N., Sparling, P. B., Healy, G. N., Dunstan, D. W., and Matthews, C. E. (2010). Sedentary behavior: Emerging Evidence for a New Health Risk. *Mayo Clinic Proceedings,* 85(12), 1138–1141. Retrieved from http://www.ncbi.nlm.nih.gov/pmc/articles/PMC2996155/

Parker, K. (2015, March 10, 2015). Despite progress, women still bear heavier load than men in balancing work and family. *FactTank: News in the Numbers.* Pew Research Center. Retrieved from http://www.pewresearch.org/fact-tank/2015/03/10/women-still-bear-heavier-load-than-men-balancing-work-family/

Pew Research Center (2010). *Millennials: A Portrait of Generation Next.* Retrieved from http://www.pewsocialtrends.org/files/2010/10/millennials-confident-connected-open-to-change.pdf

Pew Research Center (2013, December 11). Who Wants to Be the Boss? In *On Pay Gap, Millennial Women Near Parity*, Q31. Retrieved from http://www.pewsocialtrends.org/2013/12/11/on-pay-gap-millennial-women-near-parity-for-now/sdt-gender-and-work-12-2013-0-09/.

Pew Research Center: Social & Demographic Trends (2014, March 7). *Millennials in Adulthood: Detached from Institutions, Networked with Friends.* Retrieved from http://www.pewsocialtrends.org/files/2014/03/2014-03-07_generations-report-version-for-web.pdf

Popping property bubbles: Choosing the right pin. (2014, August 30). *The Economist.* Retrieved from http://www.economist.com/node/21614165/print

Rhinehart, J. B., Barrell, R. P., Dewolfe, A. S., Griffin, J. E., and Spaner, F. E. (1969). Comparative Study of Need Satisfaction in Governmental and Business Hierarchies. *Journal of Applied Psychology,* 53(3), 230–235.

S&P Capital IQ: McGraw Hill Financial (2013). *Beggar Thy Neighbor: Exploring Pension Plans Research Brief.* Retrieved from http://www.spcapitaliq.com/our-thinking/resources-ideas/Pension%20Plans%20Brief.pdf

Scisco, P., McCauley, C. D., Leslie, J. B., and Elsey, R. (2014). *Change Now! Five Steps to Better Leadership.* USA: CCL Press.

Sheehy, K. (2013, November 13). Undergrads Around the World Face Student Loan Debt. *U.S. News and World Report.* Retrieved from http://www.usnews.com/education/top-world-universities/articles/2013/11/13/undergrads-around-the-world-face-student-loan-debt

Social Security Administration (retrieved July, 2015). *Life Expectancy for Social Security*. Retrieved from https://www.ssa.gov/history/lifeexpect.html

Social Security Administration (retrieved July, 2015). *Retirement Age: Background*. Retrieved from https://www.ssa.gov/planners/retire/background.html

Student Loans Company (2012). *Full Catalogue of Official Statistics*. Retrieved from http://www.slc.co.uk/official-statistics/full-catalogue-of-official-statistics/student-loans-debt-and-repayment.aspx

Torres, N. (2014, September 18). Most People Don't Want to be Managers. *Harvard Business Review*. Retrieved from https://hbr.org/2014/09/most-people-dont-want-to-be-managers

Transamerica Center for Retirement Studies (2014). *Millennial Workers: An Emerging Generation of Super Savers*. Retrieved July 2014 from http://www.transamericacenter.org/docs/default-source/resources/center-research/tcrs2014_sr_millennials.pdf

Trawinski, L. A. (2013). *Assets and Debt across Generations: The Middle-Class Balance Sheet 1989–2010*. AARP Public Policy Institute. Retrieved from http://www.aarp.org/content/dam/aarp/research/public_policy_institute/security/2013/middle-class-balance-sheet-1989-2010-AARP-ppi-sec-pdf.pdf

The U-bend of life: Why, beyond middle age, people get happier as they get older. (2010, December 16). *The Economist*. Retrieved August 30, 2014, from http://www.economist.com/node/17722567?fsrc=scn/fb/wl/ar/ubend

United Nations, Department of Economic and Social Affairs, Population Division (2012). *World Marriage Data 2012* (POP/DB/Marr/Rev2012). Retrieved from http://www.un.org/esa/population/publications/WMD2012/MainFrame.html

Universum (2015). *Understanding a misunderstood millennial generation: Part one of a six-part series*. Retrieved from http://universumglobal.com/insights/understanding-misunderstood-generation/

Urban, Tim. (2013, September, retrieved July, 2015). *Why Generation Y Yuppies Are Unhappy*. Retrieved from http://waitbutwhy.com/2013/09/why-generation-y-yuppies-are-unhappy.html

U.S. Census Bureau (2003). Statistical abstract of the United States: 2012. Table 1337. Single Parent Households: 1980–2009. Monthly Labor Review. Retrieved from https://www.census.gov/compendia/statab/2012/tables/12s1336.pdf

U.S. Department of Health and Human Services Centers for Disease Control and Prevention (2008). *2007 National Youth Risk Behavior Survey Overview*. Retrieved August 4, 2009, from http://www.cdc.gov/HealthyYouth/yrbs/pdf/yrbs07_us_overview.pdf

Wilcox, M., and Rush, S. (2004). *The CCL Guide to Leadership in Action: How Managers and Organizations Can Improve the Practice of Leadership.* Hoboken, NJ: John Wiley & Sons.

Wild, S., Roglic, G., Green, A., Sicree, R., and King, H. (2004). Global Prevalence of Diabetes: Estimates for the year 2000 and projections for 2030. *Diabetes Care, 27*(5), 1047–1053.

World Health Organization (2004). *Work Organization and Stress: Systematic Problem Approaches for Employers, Managers and Trade Union Representatives.* World Health Organization: Protecting Workers' Health Series No 3. Retrieved from http://www.who.int/occupational_health/publications/pwh3rev.pdf

NOTES

CHAPTER 1

1. Seventy-seven percent of Millennials think having distinct reporting relationships should be important to managers. Seventy-eight percent of Millennials believe that having definite lines of authority should be important to managers.
2. Deal, J. J., Stawiski, S., Graves, L., Gentry, W. A., Weber, T. J., and Ruderman, M. (2013). Motivation at work: Which matters more, generation or managerial level? *Consulting Psychology Journal,* 65(1) (March), 1–16.
3. Rhinehart, J. B., Barrell. R. P., Dewolfe, A. S., Griffin, J. E., and Spaner, F. E. (1969). Comparative study of need satisfaction in governmental and business hierarchies. *Journal of Applied Psychology,* 53(3), 230–235.
4. Gannon, M. J., and Demler, J. W. (1971). Organizational level and job attitudes. *Psychological Reports,* 29, 399–402. Retrieved from http://www.amsciepub.com/doi/pdf/10.2466/pro.1971.29.2.399
5. Universum (2015). *Understanding a misunderstood millennial generation. Part one of a six-part series.*
6. 81 percent.
7. 35 percent.
8. 26 percent.
9. 58 percent.
10. 56 percent.
11. 29 percent.
12. Bauerlein, M. (2008). *The Dumbest Generation: How the Digital Age Stupefies Young Americans and Jeopardizes Our Future (or, Don't Trust Anyone Under 30).* London, England: Tarcher/Penguin Press.
13. 76 percent.
14. 67 percent.

CHAPTER 2

1. Hofschneider, A. (2013, September 10). Should You Bring Mom and Dad to the Office? Employers are Embracing the Involvement of Parents to Attract and Hold On to Talent. *Wall Street Journal.*

Retrieved from http://www.wsj.com/articles/SB100014241278873238 646045790669964214209866

2. Universum (2015). *Understanding a misunderstood millennial generation. Part one of a six-part series.* Retrieved from http://universumglobal.com/insights/understanding-misunderstood-generation/

3. Gardner, P. (2007). *Parent Involvement in the College Recruiting Process: To What Extent?* Retrieved from Michigan State University, Collegiate Employment Research Institute, Research Brief 2-2007, http://ceri.msu.edu/publications/pdf/ceri2-07.pdf

4. Gardner, P. (2007). *Parent involvement.*

5. Seventy-one percent of Millennials believe that parents should not visit the hiring organization during the job interview process, and an additional 20 percent are neutral.

6. Fifty-four percent of Millennials believe that the hiring organization should not send parents a copy of any offer given to their child, and an additional 31 percent are neutral.

7. Among Millennials who are married, an overwhelming majority discuss their compensation with their spouse (95 percent).

8. The Goldman Sachs Group, Inc. (2014). Millennials: The Housing Edition. In *Thematic Research.* Retrieved August 4, 2014, from http://www.thehousingrenaissance.com/resources/2014/Millennials_The_Housing_Edition_handout.pdf

9. Deal, J. J. (2007). *Retiring the Generation Gap: How Employees Young and Old Can Find Common Ground.* New York: John Wiley & Sons.

10. 74 percent.

11. Blanchard, K., and Johnson, S. (2003). *The One Minute Manager.* New York, NY: William Morrow.

12. 31 percent.

13. Blanchflower, D. G., and Oswald, A. J. (2008). Is Well-Being U-Shaped Over the Life Cycle? *Social Science & Medicine:* 66(8) (April), 1733–1749.

14. The U-bend of life: Why, beyond middle age, people get happier as they get older. (2010, December 18). *The Economist.* Retrieved August 30, 2014, from http://www.economist.com/node/17722567?fsrc=scn/fb/wl/ar/ubend

15. Pew Research Center: Social & Demographic Trends (2014, March 7). *Millennials in Adulthood: Detached from Institutions, Networked with Friends.* Retrieved from http://www.pewsocialtrends.org/files/2014/03/2014-03-07_generations-report-version-for-web.pdf

16. 61 percent.

17. 72 percent.

18. Of older employees, 44 percent say that people can be trusted, 15 percent say you can't be too careful, and 40 percent say it depends.
19. 31 percent.
20. With regard to trust, 6 percent of older respondents said they don't trust the police in their community, 31 percent said they don't trust the media, and 22 percent don't trust the banking industry. Only 24 percent say they trust people in their neighborhood or community, 43 percent say they trust people in their place of worship, and 29 percent said they trust people with whom they share religious beliefs.

CHAPTER 3

1. Per current U.S. law, when she turned 26, she would no longer be eligible for coverage under her parents' health insurance policy.
2. Feldman, D. (2013). *Inspiring the Next Generation Workforce: The 2013 Millennial Impact Report*, 23. Indianapolis, IN: Achieve Guidance. Retrieved from http://cdn.trustedpartner.com/docs/library/ AchieveMCON2013/Research%20Report/Millennial%20Impact%20 Research.pdf
3. Feldman, D. (2013). *Inspiring*, 25.
4. Feldman, D. (2013). *Inspiring*, 8.
5. Forty-two percent of female Millennials said they had looked into volunteering before the interview, in comparison with 30 percent of male Millennials. Also, 63 percent of female Millennials said that the opportunity to work for a cause made them more likely to take the job, in comparison with 45 percent of male Millennials. Feldman, D. (2013). *Inspiring*, 9.
6. Feldman, D. (2013). *Inspiring*, 18.
7. Feldman, D. (2013). *Inspiring*, 7.
8. 34 percent.
9. 54 percent.
10. 51 percent.
11. 49 percent.
12. Feldman, D. (2013). *Inspiring*, 10.
13. Friedman, T. L. (2005). *The World is Flat: A Brief History of the Twenty-First Century*. New York: Farrar, Straus, and Giroux.
14. Urban, T. (2013, September). Why Generation Y Yuppies Are Unhappy, Retrieved from http://waitbutwhy.com/2013/09/why-generation-y -yuppies-are-unhappy.html
15. Pew Research Center: Social & Demographic Trends (2014, March 7). *Millennials in Adulthood: Detached from Institutions, Networked with Friends*. Retrieved from http://www.pewsocialtrends.org/ files/2014/03/2014-03-07_generations-report-version-for-web.pdf

16. The Institute for College Access & Success (2014, November). *Student debt and the class of 2013*. Retrieved from http://ticas.org/sites/default/files/legacy/fckfiles/pub/classof2013.pdf

17. Sheehy, K. (2013, November 13). Undergrads Around the World Face Student Loan Debt. *U.S. News and World Report*. Retrieved from http://www.usnews.com/education/top-world-universities/articles/2013/11/13/undergrads-around-the-world-face-student-loan-debt

18. Popping property bubbles: Choosing the right pin. (2014, August 30). *The Economist*. Retrieved from http://www.economist.com/node/21614165/print

19. The Goldman Sachs Group, Inc. (2014). Millennials: The Housing Edition. In *Thematic Research*. Retrieved August 4, 2014, from http://www.thehousingrenaissance.com/resources/2014/Millennials_The_Housing_Edition_handout.pdf

20. Goldman Sachs Group, Inc. (2014). *Millennials*.

21. Student Loans Company (2012). *Full Catalogue of Official Statistics*. Retrieved from http://www.slc.co.uk/official-statistics/full-catalogue-of-official-statistics/student-loans-debt-and-repayment.aspx

22. Billones, C. L. (2013, March 18). Japanese students deep in debt with $5 billion in loans. *JDP*. Retrieved from http://japandailypress.com/japanese-students-deep-in-debt-with-5-billion-in-loans-1825368/

23. Deloitte Touche Tohmatsu Ltd. (2014, January 21). *Big demands and high expectations: What generation Y wants from business, government, and the future workplace*. Retrieved from http://www2.deloitte.com/uk/en/pages/press-releases/articles/big-demands-and-high-expectations-what-generation-y-wants.html

CHAPTER 4

1. Pew Research Center (2010). *Millennials: A Portrait of Generation Next*, February 25. Retrieved from http://www.pewsocialtrends.org/files/2010/10/millennials-confident-connected-open-to-change.pdf

2. Pew Research Center (2010). *Millennials*, 26.

3. Pew Research Center (2010). *Millennials*, 26.

4. Achieve Guidance (2013). *The Millennial Impact Research: The 2013 Millennial Impact Report*, 23. Retrieved from http://cdn.trustedpartner.com/docs/library/AchieveMCON2013/Research%20Report/Millennial%20Impact%20Research.pdf

5. Achieve Guidance (2013). *The 2013 Millennial Impact Report*, 23.

6. 52 percent.

7. Pew Research Center (2010). *Millennials*, 26.

8. This pattern can also be seen in Pew Research Center (2010). *Millennials: A Portrait of Generation Next, February*, 25. Retrieved

from http://www.pewsocialtrends.org/files/2010/10/millennials-confident-connected-open-to-change.pdf

9. 52 percent.
10. 73 percent.
11. 76 percent.
12. 77 percent.
13. 58 percent.
14. 74 percent.
15. Charlie Brown.
16. 26 percent.
17. 60 percent.
18. 68 percent.
19. Achieve Guidance (2013). *Inspiring the Next Generation Workforce: The 2014 Millennial Impact Report,* 14. Retrieved from http://cdn.trustedpartner.com/docs/library/AchieveMCON2013/MIR_2014.pdf
20. 42 percent.
21. 24 percent.
22. 64 percent.
23. 56 percent.
24. Ninety-three percent want performance evaluation feedback face-to-face, 95 percent want to discuss career plans face-to-face, and 84 percent want to discuss compensation face-to-face.
25. Blanchard, K., and Johnson, S. (2003). *The One Minute Manager.* New York: William Morrow. Wilcox, M., and Rush, S. (2004). *The CCL Guide to Leadership in Action: How Managers and Organizations Can Improve the Practice of Leadership.* Hoboken, NJ: John Wiley & Sons. Covey, S. M. R. (2006). *The Speed of Trust: The One Thing That Changes Everything.* New York: Free Press. Collins, J. (2011). *Good to Great.* New York: HarperCollins Publishers. Scisco, P., McCauley, C. D., Leslie, J. B., and Elsey, R. (2014). *Change Now! Five Steps to Better Leadership.* USA: CCL Press. King, S. N., Altman, D. G., and Lee, R. J. (2011). *Discovering the Leader in You: How to Realize Your Leadership Potential.* Hoboken, NJ: John Wiley & Sons.

CHAPTER 5
1. 56 percent.
2. 63 percent.
3. 61 percent.
4. 76 percent.
5. 72 percent.
6. Seventy-two percent of Millennials believe that they have access to learning and development resources at work that will help them to improve their skills.

7. Seventy-three percent of Millennials generally believe that their organization values employee learning and development.

8. Ninety-eight percent of Millennials say that developing close ties with coworkers is important to them, with 57 percent saying it is either very or extremely important to them. Sixty-six percent say they have formed strong friendships at work.

9. Fifty-eight percent of Millennials say that their immediate supervisor cares about their well-being.

10. Ninety-five percent of staff from older generations say that developing close ties with coworkers is important to them, with 43 percent saying it is either very or extremely important to them. Sixty-four percent say they have formed strong friendships at work.

11. 44 percent.

12. Pew Research Center (2013). Who Wants to Be the Boss? *On Pay Gap, Millennial Women Near Parity,* Q31. Retrieved December 11, 2013, from http://www.pewsocialtrends.org/2013/12/11/on-pay-gap-millennial-women-near-parity-for-now/sdt-gender-and-work-12-2013-0-09/

13. Universum (2015). *Understanding a misunderstood millennial generation. Part one of a six-part series.* Retrieved from http://universumglobal.com/insights/understanding-misunderstood-generation/

14. Torres, N. (2014, September 18).), Most People Don't Want to Be Managers. *Harvard Business Review.* Retrieved from https://hbr.org/2014/09/most-people-dont-want-to-be-managers

15. Specifically, 30 percent say they often think about quitting their present job, and 25 percent say they are looking for another job right now. Though many say they aren't currently looking for a new job, 36 percent say they will probably look for a new job in the near future, and 27 percent say that they are planning to look for a job outside their organization in the next year.

16. The longer the time period, the smaller the percentage of Millennials who say they intend to continue working for their current employer. Seventy-eight percent say they intend to be working for their organization in six months; 67 percent say they intend to be working for their organization in one year; 39 percent say they intend to be working for their organization in five years.

17. 47 percent.

18. Twenty-six percent don't feel their supervisors are supportive, 23 percent say that their managers don't appreciate it when they put in extra effort, 26 percent don't believe their managers are forgiving of honest mistakes, and 31 percent don't think their managers understand when they have to prioritize their life over work.

19. 70 percent.
20. 63 percent.
21. Pew Research Center (2010). *Millennials: A portrait of generation next* 41. Retrieved from http://www.pewsocialtrends.org/files/2010/10/ millennials-confident-connected-open-to-change.pdf
22. 63 percent.
23. 32 percent.
24. 70 percent.
25. 76 percent.
26. 73 percent.
27. 72 percent.
28. 54 percent.
29. 63 percent.
30. 77 percent.
31. 68 percent.
32. 61 percent.
33. 28 percent.
34. 55 percent.

CHAPTER 6

1. Chura, H. (2006, April 22). Sabbaticals Aren't Just for Academics Anymore. *New York Times*. Retrieved from http://www.nytimes .com/2006/04/22/business/22sabbaticals.html

CHAPTER 7

1. Kahn, L. B. (2010). The long-term labor market consequences of graduating from college in a bad Economy. *Labour Economics, 17*(2), 303–316. Oreopoulos, P., von Wachter, T., and Heisz, A. (2006, April). The short- and long-term career effects of graduating in a recession: Hysteresis and heterogeneity in the market for college graduates. National Bureau of Economic Research Working Paper no. 12159. Retrieved from http://www.nber.org/papers/w12159
2. The research on long-term impacts of recessions was conducted based on people graduating in recessions in the 1980s and 1990s, which had a much milder impact on college graduates than the Great Recession of 2007–08. We expect the Great Recession to have deeper and longer-lasting impacts on the Millennials than the two previous recessions had on the Gen Xers who graduated at that time.
3. The expansion of the early 2000s and subsequent deep recession starting in 2008 characterized the experience of Millennials in most of the developed countries in our data, primarily in the United States,

the United Kingdom, and Europe. However, the degree of expansion and then contraction varied across countries within this group. The experience in the developing countries was different. For example, China's growth slowed but never came close to an economic contraction.

4. Social Security Administration. *Life Expectancy for Social Security.* Retrieved July 2015 from http://www.ssa.gov/history/lifeexpect .html

5. Social Security Administration. *Retirement Age: Background.* Retrieved July 2015 from http://www.ssa.gov/retirement/background .html

6. S&P Capital IQ: McGraw Hill Financial (2013). *Beggar Thy Neighbor: Exploring Pension Plans Research Brief.* Retrieved from http:// www.spcapitaliq.com/our-thinking/resources-ideas/Pension%20 Plans%20Brief.pdf

7. McHugh, D. (2013, December 29). The Convergence Of 3 Factors Is Driving A Worldwide Retirement Crisis. *Business Insider.* Retrieved from http://www.businessinsider.com/worldwide-retirement-crisis-coming-2013-12

8. Transamerica Center for Retirement Studies (2014). *Millennial Workers: An Emerging Generation of Super Savers.* Retrieved July 2014 from http://www.transamericacenter.org/docs/default-source /resources/center-research/tcrs2014_sr_millennials.pdf

9. Levenson, A. (2006). Trends in Job and Wages in the U.S. Economy. In Lawler, E. E., and O'Toole, J., eds., *America at Work: Choices and Challenges*, 87–107. New York: Palgrave MacMillan. Mishel, L., Bernstein, J., and Allegretto, S. (2005). *The State of Working America 2004/2005.* Ithaca, NY: ILR Press. Atkinson, A. B., Piketty, T., and Saez, E. (2011). Top Incomes in the Long Run of History. *Journal of Economic Literature*, 49(1), 3–71. Gottschalk, P., and Joyce, M. (1998). Cross-National Differences in the Rise in Earnings Inequality: Market and Institutional Factors. *The Review of Economics and Statistics*, 80(4), 489–502. Lemieux, T. (2006). Increasing Residual Wage Inequality: Composition Effects, Noisy Data, or Rising Demand for Skill? *American Economic Review*, 96(3), 461–498.

10. The College Board (2014). *Trends in College Pricing 2014.* Retrieved from http://trends.collegeboard.org/college-pricing. Lorin, J. (2014, November 12). College tuition in the U.S. Again Rises Faster Than Inflation. *Bloomberg Business.* Retrieved from http://www.bloomberg.com/news/articles/2014-11-13/ college-tuition-in-the-u-s-again-rises-faster-than-inflation

11. Olson, E. (2014, September 13). Student Loan Debt Burdens More Than Just Young People. *New York Times*. Retrieved from http://www.nytimes.com/2014/09/13/business/student-loan-debt-burdens-more-than-just-young-people.html

12. Trawinski, L. A. (2013). *Assets and Debt Across Generations: The middle-class balance sheet 1989–2010*. AARP Public Policy Institute. Retrieved from http://www.aarp.org/content/dam/aarp/research/public_policy_institute/security/2013/middle-class-balance-sheet-1989-2010-AARP-ppi-sec-pdf.pdf

13. Centers for Disease Control and Prevention (2014). *Child Obesity Facts. Obesity in Adolescents Aged 12–19 Increased from 5 percent in 1980 to 21 percent in 2012*. Retrieved February 10, 2015, from http://www.cdc.gov/healthyyouth/obesity/facts.htm

14. U.S. Department of Health and Human Services Centers for Disease Control and Prevention (2008). *2007 National Youth Risk Behavior Survey Overview*. Retrieved August 4, 2009, from http://www.cdc.gov/HealthyYouth/yrbs/pdf/yrbs07_us_overview.pdf

15. McGill, H. C., Jr., McMahan, C. A., and Gidding, S. S. (2008). Preventing Heart Disease in the 21st Century: Implications of the Pathobiological Determinants of Atherosclerosis in Youth (PDAY) Study. *Circulation*, 117(9), 1216–1227.

16. Wild, S., Roglic, G., Green, A., Sicree, R., and King, H. (2004). Global Prevalence of Diabetes: Estimates for the year 2000 and projections for 2030. *Diabetes Care*, 27(5), 1047–1053.

17. Hossain, P., Kawar, B., and El Nahas, M. (2007). Obesity and Diabetes in the Developing World—A Growing Challenge. *New England Journal of Medicine*, 356(3), 213–215.

18. Wild, S., Roglic, G., Green, A., Sicree, R., and King, H. (2004). Global Prevalence of Diabetes: Estimates for the year 2000 and projections for 2030. *Diabetes Care*, 27(5), 1047–1053.

19. Barkin, S. L., Heerman, W. J., Warren, M. D., and Rennhoff, C. (2010). Millennials and the world of work: The impact of obesity on health and productivity. *Journal of Business and Psychology*, 25(2), 239–245.

20. Baum, C. L., II, and Ford, W. F. (2004). The Wage Effects of Obesity: A Longitudinal Study. *Health Economics*, 3(9), 885–899. Retrieved from http://amosyang.net/wp-content/uploads/2012/10/wageobesity.pdf

21. Finkelstein, E., Fiebelkorn, C., and Wang, G. (2005). The Costs of Obesity Among Full-Time Employees. *American Journal of Health Promotion*, 20(1), 45–51.

22. Kelly, T., Yang, W., Chen, C.-S., Reynolds, K., and He, J. (2008). Global Burden of Obesity in 2005 and Projections to 2030. *International Journal of Obesity*, 32, 1431–1437. Retrieved from http://www.nature.com/ijo/journal/v32/n9/full/ijo2008102a.html

23. Owen, N., Sparling, P. B., Healy, G. N., Dunstan, D. W., and Matthews, C. E. (2010). Sedentary behavior: Emerging Evidence for a New Health Risk. *Mayo Clinic Proceedings*, 85(12), 1138–1141. Retrieved from http://www.ncbi.nlm.nih.gov/pmc/articles/PMC2996155/

24. World Health Organization (2004). *Work Organization and Stress: Systematic Problem Approaches for Employers, Managers and Trade Union Representatives*. World Health Organization: Protecting Workers' Health Series No 3. 2. Retrieved from http://www.who.int/occupational_health/publications/pwh3rev.pdf

25. American Psychological Association (2015). *Stress in America: Paying with Our Health*. Retrieved from http://www.apa.org/news/press/releases/stress/2014/stress-report.pdf

26. American Psychological Association (2014). *Stress in America: Are Teens Adopting Adults' Stress Habits?* Retrieved from https://www.apa.org/news/press/releases/stress/2013/stress-report.pdf

27. American Psychological Association (2015). *Stress in America: Paying With Our Health.*

28. Ibid.

29. Ibid.

30. United Nations, Department of Economic and Social Affairs, Population Division (2012). *World Marriage Data 2012* (POP/DB/Marr/Rev2012). Retrieved from http://www.un.org/esa/population/publications/WMD2012/MainFrame.html

31. The Goldman Sachs Group, Inc. (2014). Millennials: The Housing Edition. In *Thematic Research*. Retrieved August 4, 2014, from http://www.thehousingrenaissance.com/resources/2014/Millennials_The_Housing_Edition_handout.pdf

32. U.S. Census Bureau (2003). Statistical abstract of the United States: 2012. Table 1337. Single Parent Households: 1980–2009. Monthly Labor Review. Retrieved from https://www.census.gov/compendia/statab/2012/tables/12s1336.pdf

33. Harvard Business School (2015, May). *Life & Leadership After HBS: Findings*. Retrieved from http://www.hbs.edu/women50/docs/L_and_L_Survey_2Findings_12final.pdf

34. Parker, K. (2015). Despite progress, women still bear heavier load than men in balancing work and family. *FactTank: News in the Numbers*. Pew Research Center. Retrieved March 10, 2015, from http://www.pewresearch.org/fact-tank/2015/03/10/women-still-bear-heavier-load-than-men-balancing-work-family/

INDEX

ABOUT THE AUTHORS

Jennifer J. Deal is a Senior Research Scientist at the Center for Creative Leadership (CCL©) in San Diego, California, an Affiliated Research Scientist at the Center for Effective Organizations at the University of Southern California, and a contributor to the *Wall Street Journal*'s "Experts" panel on leadership. Her research focuses on global leadership and generational differences and has been featured in numerous academic and business publications, and in the *Wall Street Journal*, the *New York Times, The Guardian, The Economist, Strategy&, Forbes*, the *Associated Press, CNN, National Public Radio, South China Morning Post*, the *Globe and Mail*, and *Training Development* magazine.

She is the manager of CCL's World Leadership Survey and the Emerging Leaders research project. In 2002 she coauthored *Success for the New Global Manager* (Jossey-Bass/Wiley Publishers), and she has published articles on generational issues, the strategic use of information in negotiation, executive selection, cultural adaptability, global management, and women in management. Her second book, *Retiring the Generation Gap*, was published in 2007. An internationally recognized expert on generational differences, she has spoken on the topic on six continents (North and South America, Europe, Asia, Africa, and Australia).

She holds a BA in psychology from Haverford College and an MA and PhD in industrial/organizational psychology with a specialty in political psychology from the Ohio State University.

Alec Levenson is an Economist and Senior Research Scientist at the Center for Effective Organizations, Marshall School of Business, University of Southern California. His action research and consulting work with companies optimize job and organization performance and HR systems, focusing on the following:

- Organizational and talent strategies for emerging markets and global organizations
- Talent management practices for the new generation of workers and world of work
- Human capital analytics to improve decisions around talent
- Organization design and effectiveness

His work with companies combines the best elements of scientific research and practical, actionable knowledge that companies can use to improve performance. He draws from the disciplines of economics, strategy, organization behavior, and industrial/organizational psychology to tackle complex talent and organizational challenges that defy easy solutions. His recommendations focus on the actions organizations should take to make lasting improvements in critical areas.

He has trained HR professionals from a broad range of Fortune 500 and Global 500 companies in human capital analytics. He has authored two previous books, *Employee Surveys That Work: Improving Design, Use, and Organizational Impact* and *Strategic Analytics: Advancing Strategy Execution and Organizational Effectiveness.*

His research has been featured in numerous academic and business publications and in the *New York Times*, the *Wall Street Journal*, *The Economist*, *CNN*, *BusinessWeek*, the *Associated Press*, *U.S. News and World Report*, *National Public Radio*, the *Los Angeles Times*, *USA Today*, *Marketplace*, *Fox News*, and many other news outlets.

He received his PhD and MA in economics from Princeton University, specializing in labor economics and development economics, and his BA in economics and Chinese language from the University of Wisconsin–Madison.

ABOUT THE CENTER FOR CREATIVE LEADERSHIP

The Center for Creative Leadership (CCL) is a top-ranked, global provider of leadership development. By leveraging the power of leadership to drive results that matter most to clients, CCL transforms individual leaders, teams, organizations, and society. Its array of cutting-edge solutions is steeped in extensive research and experience gained from working with hundreds of thousands of leaders at all levels. Ranked among the world's top five providers of executive education by the *Financial Times* and in the top 10 by *Bloomberg BusinessWeek*, CCL has offices in Greensboro, NC; Colorado Springs, CO; San Diego, CA; Brussels, Belgium; Moscow, Russia; Addis Ababa, Ethiopia; Johannesburg, South Africa; Singapore; Gurgaon, India; and Shanghai, China.

ABOUT THE CENTER FOR EFFECTIVE ORGANIZATIONS

The Center for Effective Organizations (CEO) in the Marshall School of Business at the University of Southern California is internationally recognized for over three decades of outstanding research and thought leadership. CEO actively involves companies in its action research, yielding practical, data-based knowledge, and works with them to design and implement changes that improve effectiveness. CEO Research Scientists apply the principles of organization design, complex change theory, HR metrics and analytics, strategy analysis, leadership, and talent management to improve how organizations operate. CEO is also widely recognized for its exceptional executive education and learning programs in all areas of human capital and organizational effectiveness.